Barriers to Excellence is dedicated to all those who choose to make our world a better place, and especially to two friends who have done just that with their lives.
Michael A. Noonan (1940-2010)
F. G. (Bob) Doucette (1940-2012)

"We have a choice to use the gift of our lives to make the world a better place."

—Jane Goodall

Barriers to Excellence

The Changes Needed for Our Schools

Betsy Gunzelmann

ROWMAN & LITTLEFIELD EDUCATION
A division of
ROWMAN & LITTLEFIELD PUBLISHERS, INC.
Lanham • New York • Toronto • Plymouth, UK

Published by Rowman & Littlefield Education
A division of Rowman & Littlefield Publishers, Inc.
A wholly owned subsidary of The Rowman & Littlefield Publishing Group, Inc.
4501 Forbes Boulevard, Suite 200, Lanham, Maryland 20706
www.rowman.com

10 Thornbury Road, Plymouth PL6 7PP, United Kingdom

British Library Cataloguing in Publication Information Available

Library of Congress Cataloging-in-Publication Data

Gunzelmann, Betsy, 1952-
Barriers to excellence : the changes needed for our schools / Betsy Gunzelmann. pages cm
pages cm.
Includes bibliographical references and index.
ISBN 978-1-61048-578-4 (cloth : alk. paper) -- ISBN 978-1-61048-579-1 (pbk. : alk. paper) -- ISBN
978-1-61048-580-7 (electronic) (print)
1. School improvement programs--United States. 2. Educational change--United States. I. Title.
LB2822.82.G86 2012
371.2'07--dc23

2012010466

The paper used in this publication meets the minimum requirements of American National
Standard for Information Sciences Permanence of Paper for Printed Library Materials,
ANSI/NISO Z39.48-1992.

Printed in the United States of America

Contents

Acknowledgments

My interest in the crossroads between the fields of psychology and education has been with me throughout my thirty-plus-year career. Understanding people, assessment and testing, learning, treatment intervention, social environments, organizational issues, and research are all within the range of skills of a psychologist, and are all quite essential to improving our schools. I also am trained as an educator and have studied, researched, and been involved in education for many years.

I feel truly privileged for the many people who have been influential with their encouragement, support, and belief in the importance of getting the message out regarding the barriers preventing excellence in our schools. First and foremost, I want to thank Dean Karen Erickson for her support at Southern New Hampshire University. Also, my research students at SNHU who are mentioned individually within the text deserve a special thank you.

My college-age son also merits recognition; he keeps me inspired by his motivation for academic excellence and his belief in my work. He is also a great proofreader.

A special thank you is extended to Tom Koerner, vice president at Rowman & Littlefield Education, for his continued confidence in my writing. Thanks also to Carlie Wall for her production work, turning the manuscript into the finished product. Without a doubt the entire team at Rowman & Littlefield is outstanding.

Preface

At times it seems as if we are just butting our heads against a brick wall when it comes to attaining educational excellence in the United States. Why is it that our students' achievement has, for the most part, shown a decline for the last several decades? Why is it that we no longer are the world leaders in education? Why is it that we are one of the most inequitable countries educationally of all of the industrialized countries in the world? Why is it that we seem to have one educational policy after another that does not address our educational problems? Why is it that we use testing in a manner that is unreliable, invalid, and not helpful?

These and other questions will be answered in *Barriers to Excellence*, which brings a different way of looking at our educational problems.

Part I

Our Broken System: Understanding Barriers to Excellence

Chapter One

There Is Trouble in Our Schools: A Historical Overview of Barriers and Imbalance

Our schools are in trouble. You may have heard this before, but you may not realize how serious the problem really is. The United States used to lead the world in education . . . but we have been gradually and consistently trailing behind many other countries. If we do not begin to break down the barriers to educational excellence and rebalance our educational system, the long-term ramifications of this decline will affect our country's capacity to maintain our leadership ability and competitive edge.

During the late 1950s the United States became concerned when the Soviet Union first sent Sputnik into space, scoring the advantage for Soviet missile ability and intensifying the Cold War and the nuclear arms race. Such political, scientific, and technological events had definite ramifications for the United States educational system.

President Kennedy confronted the American education structure, requiring an enhanced math and science emphasis for our students. Additionally, the U.S. Office of Education had just issued a report on the state of American education estimating that in science, Soviet students were about two years ahead of U.S. students. University researchers became more closely involved in the development of school science curricula (United States History, 2012).

During the 1970s the United States lead the world in education, but during the 1980s many of programs were cut and the gains were lost. Progress was again made during the 1990s, but not enough, as other countries soared ahead with well-researched, well-planned, and well-funded educational agendas. The most recent Program for International Student Assessment: PISA results place U.S. students in the middle of the pack of participating countries in science and reading literacy and below average in mathematics.

Numerous countries are soaring above the United States academically, including Finland, South Korea, Canada, the Netherlands, and Japan, which were among the top ten. Although it was Shanghai, China's first time taking the PISA, its students scored the highest of all countries in all areas (Paine & Schleicher, 2011).

We can learn a lot from these other countries, especially Finland as Dr. Sahlberg (2010) points out in Finnish Lessons. Clearly, the approaches of competition, test-based accountability and performance-based pay have not worked well and have been found to be counterproductive and unnecessary within the Finnish system. Yet, we also must keep in mind that our educational problems are, in many ways, unique to the United States.

It is important to understand that our schools are in trouble, not just because of some scores on a particular test or because the United States is no longer in first place and leading the world in education. The real problems lie with the numerous barriers that are preventing excellence in our students.

These barriers are complex and widespread but unquestionably will impact the future of our country if we do not take heed and address the problems. So clearly, there has never been a better time or an era of greater need than now for understanding the barriers preventing excellence in education for the twenty-first century.

We are at a crossroad where our faltering educational system could continue to decline. Either our children will not be prepared to compete in our global society or we can break down the barriers preventing excellence in our schools and ensure that our children can continue to prosper, contribute, and lead. The choice should be obvious, but the remedy is not as apparent.

We should always remember to look back over the course of history to prevent repeating mistakes and to thwart the construction of unnecessary boundaries. Boundaries stop us from going further . . . they do this with learning, too. As Columbus discovered, the world does not end at the horizon, and nothing disastrous happened when he kept on sailing. In fact, a whole new world was opened up. So, too, with learning: boundaries can prevent us from excelling, or we can be courageous and make new discoveries.

Yet it seems we are so afraid of boundaries. Possibly the fear is based upon a perceived loss of control. Such anxiety is understandable, only human, really. However, as with all anxiety we must ask whether the fear is reasonable or is getting in the way of our ultimate objective—in this case, our goal of educational excellence for all.

President Ronald Reagan was well aware of the limitations of boundaries placed before us when he said, "Tear down this wall!" in Berlin back on June 12, 1987 (Reagan, 1987). Walls separate people, block communication, and suppress learning and the exchange of ideas. Our educational boundaries are not made from concrete, brick, or even barbed wire.

Many of our boundaries cannot be seen with the naked eye; nonetheless, they exist and they prevent excellence. Certainly we are not walled in as the Germans were with the Berlin Wall. Yet these toxic walls block learning. Our boundaries are much more inconspicuous, so understated that many do not even perceive them as walls . . . but they are indeed!

In 2008, then presidential candidate Barack Obama spoke in Germany and again mentioned the need to tear down the walls that separate all people so that common world problems, including global warming, nuclear threats, terrorism, AIDS, poverty, and genocide, can be solved (Obama, 2008). Since taking office, President Obama has made education one of his top priorities for he is well aware of the educational decline of many of our U.S. students.

TYPES OF BARRIERS PREVENTING EDUCATIONAL EXCELLENCE FOR THE TWENTY-FIRST CENTURY

Many types of toxic barriers prevent excellence. I'll describe several of them here, and as we become more advanced in our understanding, we may discover others not even on the radar at this time. For example, *societal/cultural barriers*, which involve our shared, common ideals. *Cultural barriers* really are a subset under our societal values and involve the improvement of the mind through arts and manners as I am using the definition here. I'm not saying there is anything wrong with our ideals . . . just that the pendulum has swung too far and a rebalancing is in order, and perhaps an expanding of ideals as well.

Political Barriers

Political Barriers also impact our educational systems significantly as we shall see. It is not that our government is not trying, each new administration attempts to make needed changes. Yet it seem that our politicians are not expert at educational reform and may not always be listening to the needed changes that can work and be sustainable.

There are *economic and racial boundaries*, too. (Each of these areas will be addressed separately as well). In traditional schooling, children are confined to make do with the learning materials and books available within their school building or district. Many schools are notoriously underfunded for books. Some educators are afraid to use the books lest they become damaged. Children from poorer communities with higher rates of minority students often have fewer resources. This form of discrimination and inequity must change.

Psychological Barriers

Then there are several *psychological barriers*. *Cognitive boundaries* are potential psychological barriers that involve how our thoughts can limit our learning. For example, believing that we do not need to learn the languages of others, as many in the United States believe, prevents us from fully understanding other cultures and ways of being. Such language limitations put us at a huge disadvantage in negotiations.

Furthermore, we may well be misunderstood by others and perceived as arrogant. This is a very damaging and limiting boundary. Many of our cognitive boundaries are deeply ingrained in our Western cultural beliefs. It can be difficult for us to fully understand the perspective of people from different countries because of our cognitive boundaries . . . of course, the reverse may be true as well.

This brings us to the topic of *emotional boundaries*. Emotional boundaries prevent us from taking risks, from going beyond our regular comfort zones to deepen our understanding. Fear and anxiety often underlie such barriers. Isolating ourselves, avoiding opportunities, valuing uniqueness, and deceiving ourselves into believing we are right are all barriers to learning.

Truly becoming an educated person involves learning to take such emotional risks to get involved outside of our narrow and biased perspective. Why not experience the cultures of others by becoming concerned citizens of the world? World travel may not be available to all, but certainly the world news is . . . along with seeing it from the perspective of those from other nations. For example, why not watch the world news from a European, Mideastern, Asian, or African country?

Of course, there will be bias from different perspectives . . . but so, too, is there bias from our news reporters because they are human, and we are all subject to bias. Isn't this part of becoming an educated person . . . to learn to sort through these reported "truths" to reach a deeper understanding and appreciation of one another?

Boundaries to motivation: Yes, there are roadblocks interfering with motivation in the United States as well. Many students want to "fit in," to be a part of their school community. Yet in many parts of our culture, in many schools and classrooms, it just is not cool to be smart. The media plays right into this unfortunate development, portraying the "jocks," the leading actors in movies, and music idols as individuals who scoff at scholars. In reality, some of the best, most talented stars are well-rounded intellectuals.

Motivation issues may impact teachers as well, particularly when they are underpaid and not fully valued for the important work they do. Furthermore, the day-to-day work of teachers is difficult, and many believe they are not adequately trained for the work they are required to achieve.

Physical Barriers

There are *physical boundaries* to learning, too. Traditional schooling requires a school building. Early American schools were often referred to as schoolhouses and might consist of one room, with grades grouped together and boys and girls entering and exiting through separate doorways. In the United States we've made some progress with our buildings, but now many are old and in need of remediation and updating. Often, school buildings are overcrowded, with far too many children in one classroom for optimal learning to occur.

Yet there may be less worry about the size of a classroom when we consider the world as our classroom. Schools and school rooms can be as large or as small as needed; technology can adjust to the needs of the community. In very remote areas near K2, in the mountainous regions of Afghanistan, it is very difficult to get building materials to build schools. Through technology, children, even in these most desolate areas, can have access to a world-class education. (What a wonderful way to mend some of the fences that have been so seriously damaged in that part of the world.)

So, too, we can tear down the barriers to learning that so many children experience who are labeled with disorders that affect learning, including children with a variety of learning disabilities, autism, mental retardation, anxiety disorders, depression, attention deficit disorder, and physical disabilities. With a broader approach, students will have access to highly individualized programs from premier professionals and to leading teachers and therapists. Additionally, with the proper technology, they may have the opportunity to learn equally as well as their classmates. They will no longer be limited educationally.

Time boundaries also interfere with educational excellence and come in many forms. Learning can and does occur at any time, summer or winter, day or night. Real, in-depth learning has no beginning or ending time. When students are truly engaged in learning, time does not matter, except that often the feeling is that there is not enough time.

The *boundary of age* is yet another type of time boundary. Ageism should not apply to learning. Learning can and does happen at all ages. Therefore, education should not be seen as something that happens to children up to a certain age, but as a process that begins at birth and continues throughout the life span.

The twelve to sixteen years of typical formal education puts unnecessary limits on our thinking of what real learning is about. It sets the tone for learning in a negative light. It is often seen as something that must be endured, a task we must get out of the way before we can get on with life. This negative thought process sets an attitude for mediocrity, not for excellence. The limitation of a specific time for learning also shortchanges the depth of learning students could obtain without such unnecessary restraints and often does not allow time for reflection, to think about what one is learning.

NEED FOR BALANCE

Clearly, there are many barriers impacting educational excellence . . . but the issues become barriers only when there is an imbalance in the system. As we go through each of the barriers in more depth in the upcoming chapters, I hope to show how these barriers can be brought back into balance . . . allowing for educational excellence once again. We need to challenge our thinking, redefine our policies, break down our outdated, ineffective boundaries, and rebalance our educational system for excellence.

THE TIME IS ALSO RIGHT

The time is also right for tearing down boundaries and rebalancing because we are at a defining moment, with technological development advancing at an astonishing rate. Microsoft founder Bill Gates also believes that education is the key to helping the United States renew its excellence and believes that it can have a worldwide impact (Gates & Mundie, 2007). The broader focus makes perfect sense in order to bring the education of Americans to a level of excellence.

Gates also talks about the current accessibility of technology and the expected gains over the next ten years, creating even more possibilities for a truly global education. He also believes that the cost of such technology will be more affordable (Gates & Mundie, 2007). Then we will be able to reach all people—learning about one another, expanding ideas, a real education without boundaries.

We are on the cusp of where others could only dream. With all that is available and in the process of development, there are no limits to how far we will be able to progress; there are no boundaries to our potential for growth, for learning. Hillary Clinton was really onto something with her famous African quote, "It takes a village to raise a child," but really it should read, "It takes a world to educate a child." Educated children of the future are children of the world, knowledgeable, skilled, and most of all, thoughtful and living in harmony. How exciting, captivating, motivating when we truly can say the world is our classroom.

There's no time like the present. So let's get moving on understanding the need for global education and ways that we can implement true learning, learning with balance and without boundaries for excellence.

Today's real borders are not between nations, but between powerful and powerless, free and fettered, privileged and humiliated. Today, no walls can separate humanitarian or human rights crises in one part of the world from national security crises in another.
—Kofi A. Annan

Chapter Two

Rescuing Our Schools

Perspectives of Leaders, Reformers, and Entrepreneurs

The United States really is quite a remarkable country, and we have many outstanding educators, scientists, researchers, and academic institutions. We have grown so quickly in many areas (scientifically, technologically, industrially, etc.), and many discoveries have been made by specific individuals schooled in our classrooms. So, one might ask, "Doesn't that prove that we are doing a good job educating our youth?"

The answer is a definite "no" . . . since many more children are falling behind academically. Numerous children do not do as well as they could and find themselves unprepared for higher education. It is these individuals I am most concerned with, and indeed it is the majority of our youth.

The biggest problem we face is that there is not a consensus as to just what the problems are, what causes the problems, and how to go about rescuing our schools. Back in 1983, the U.S. Department of Education released a momentous report, *A Nation at Risk*. At that time it was determined that 13 percent of seventeen-year-olds were functionally illiterate, scores were declining on the SAT (Scholastic Aptitude Test), and many students were in need of remedial courses at the college level. The U.S. Department of Education released a follow-up report titled *A Nation Accountable*. Twenty-five years later, it seems we are even more at risk (U.S. Department of Education, 2008). In this more current report, the authors state:

> Fortunately, thanks to the recent standards and accountability movement and the *No Child Left Behind Act*, we are finally taking an honest, comprehensive look at our schools. For the first time in our country's history, we have reliable data to evaluate student performance and address weaknesses in our schools. (p. 1)

Unfortunately, there are several problems with the above statement. There are several reasons why the standards, the accountability movement, NCLB, and current assessment practices have created barriers which are actually inhibiting excellence.

Dr. Deborah Meier at NYU eloquently expresses the "dark side" of "standards-based" reform in American education. She believes that standards can mask and make way for other agendas: punishing kids, privatizing public education, giving up on equity. Meier goes on to say:

> Even in the hands of sincere allies of children, equity, and public education, the current push for far greater standardization than we've ever previously attempted is fundamentally misguided. It will not help to develop young minds, contribute to a robust democratic life, or aid the most vulnerable of our fellow citizens. By shifting the locus of authority to outside bodies, it undermines the capacity of schools to instruct by example in the qualities of mind that schools in a democracy should be fostering in kids—responsibility for one's own ideas, tolerance for the ideas of others, and a capacity to negotiate differences. (Meier, 2011)

Dr. Meier is correct, but possibly we need to also consider the helpful side of standards. We want our children to have high standards. Thus standards are not actually the problem . . . but it is the way they are used and misused that result in failure.

An important clarifying quote from Dr. Jonathan Kozol helps to put this issue into perspective:

> So the question, for me, isn't if we ought to have "standards" in our children's education. It is, rather, how and where they are determined, and by whom, and how they're introduced, and how we treat and penalize (or threaten, or abuse) the child or teacher who won't swallow them. (Kozol, 2000, p. x)

E. D. Hirsch takes a different slant in *The Knowledge Deficit: Closing the Shocking Education Gap for American Children* (2006). Hirsch speaks of the need for core knowledge and cultural literacy. Reading is at the core of learning and communication ability, allowing the reader to gain new information rapidly, and is also at the core of a democratic education.

Legendary educator John Holt (1964) described in his book *How Children Fail* the reasons why bright children are not performing well in our schools and how our schools fail our children. Holt's writing demonstrates the long-term academic problems faced by our nation and that they affect many of our most capable students.

Pioneering educator and activist Jonathan Kozol (1991) exposed the deplorable conditions of inequities in our schools. Such imbalances rob children of their rights to education and deprive us all of their lost potential. Our schools are still far from equitable; indeed, they are the most inequitable of those in any of the industrialized nations. For years, educator and journalist John Merrow has reported on the problems in our schools in his PBS Series *The Merrow Report* and his book *Choosing Excellence: Good Enough Schools Are Not Good Enough.* When writing of mediocre schools, Merrow states: "These are the schools we accept, even though we know our children deserve better" (Merrow, 2001, p. xv).

Another leading educational expert points out that the educational needs of our children have changed, but our schools have not kept pace. Dr. Wagner states: "Our system of public education—our curricula, teaching methods, and the tests we require students to take—were created in a different century for the needs of another era. They are hopelessly outdated" (Wagner, 2008, p. 9).

Such commentaries go on and on, each making an important point. None are really incorrect; each is attempting to wake up the American people to the need to rescue our schools. Yet each seems to hold only a piece of the puzzle without any idea of the overall picture. The ramifications for our country are frightening and hit at the core of democracy. We have lost our competitive edge as a world leader in education.

Being first and best is not the real issue at stake; it is losing the competitive edge which impacts all of our ability to thrive in the global economic market and erodes the core belief system of our society. (More about this in chapter 4.) Our children are facing international competition for acceptance into institutions of higher education, a global economic crisis, high unemployment rates, and extreme competition for available jobs. They are losing out to other better educated, better prepared students.

Back in 2007, then senator Obama commented on these very issues.

> This is a defining moment for our generation. Revolutions in communications and technology have created a global economy of high-tech, high-wage jobs that can be located anywhere there's an internet connection—an economy where the most valuable skill you can sell is your knowledge.
> Education is now the currency of the Information Age. It's no longer just a pathway to opportunity and success—it's a prerequisite. (Obama, 2007)

President Barack Obama is still concerned and making strides toward addressing inequality in our schools and the educational declines seen over the years. He understands the importance for our children and for our country . . . and he will try to put together all of the pieces for educational excellence . . . but a broader understanding is essential.

Microsoft founder Bill Gates also is concerned. "When we looked at the millions of students that our high schools were not preparing for higher education and we looked at the damaging impact that it has on their lives— we came to a painful conclusion: America's high schools are obsolete" (Gates, 2005).

Gates has addressed Congress on more than one occasion about the difficulty of hiring well-qualified U.S. students for high-paying jobs in his field. Many of the jobs are going to better educated foreign students (Gates, 2008).

RESCUING OUR SCHOOLS AND SAVING OUR COUNTRY

The fact that our schools need rescuing is clear. The reasons for this crisis are less so, complicated by our changing world. However, by breaking down the barriers to educational excellence and balancing our educational system we can help our young people (the future of our country) to attain educational excellence and make our country even greater, stronger, and more helpful to those in need.

In *Hidden Dangers: Subtle Signs of Failing Schools* and in *Hidden Dangers to Kids' Learning* we learned of many dangers which sabotage our children's learning and can be addressed by our teachers, administrators, and parents on an individual and school-by-school basis. This is important, but not the entire picture.

These dangers are embedded in a larger scheme made up of the barriers preventing excellence. It is these barriers which are more difficult to understand and thus to change. It is these barriers which become unbalanced and can wreak short-term havoc on our children's education and cause long-term destruction to our country's distinction.

Alfie Kohn (2008) has a good point in his article, "Beware School 'Reformers'" . . . although he may miss the mark with the need for broader understanding requiring a team approach to education reform. Yes, we do indeed need an educator running the Education Department, but we also need input from a variety of other experts since education impacts all aspects of our country. Indeed, the loudest voice must be from educators well versed in qualitative and quantitative research with the expertise to apply such understanding accurately.

Our current U.S. secretary of education, Arne Duncan, says many of the right words . . . but he, too, needs to look more broadly and rely on the expertise from many disciplines when he says such things as referring to education as "the most pressing issue facing America," "[P]reparing young people for success in life is not just a moral obligation of society" . . . but an "economic imperative," and "Education is also the civil rights issue of our generation."

Duncan goes on to resolve in his confirmation hearing "to enhance education in America, to lift our children out of poverty, to help our students learn to contribute to the civility of our great American democracy, and to strengthen the economy by producing a workforce that can make us as competitive as possible" (Duncan, 2009).

Here we are in 2011, and it is apparent that Mr. Duncan may have been focusing too heavily on certain issues without that broader perspective that is essential for real and permanent change to occur, for the barriers to educational distinction to be fully understood, torn down when necessary, or in most cases brought back into balance to allow our true excellence to be realized.

So clearly, we need to look more broadly than just the subtle yet specific dangers to educational excellence, yet we will not forget to look at the more specific issues involved with attaining a true education. Indeed, education is impacted by all aspects of our country and in turn will impact all aspects of our country. Undeniably, education is the most pressing issue facing the United States today. The state of the union is in educational turmoil: it is time to rescue our schools and save our country!

Gathering data from many directions was the beginning of the rescue effort. The process is described in chapter 3.

Chapter Three

The Gathering of Data from Many Directions

The gathering of information for *Barriers to Excellence* comes from a variety of resources and even references from different parts of the world. The process was time consuming, to say the least; at times it seemed a bit overwhelming, but always fascinating. I must say I even felt driven to get the messages out to the public as quickly as possible, for as you shall see, we have no time left to waste.

If changes are not made to improve the education of our youth in the United States, we will be unable to maintain our role in the global society as a world leader. We have already lost our edge as a world leader in education in many ways. Our children are scoring much lower on the PISA . . . a test that is not a typical multiple-choice assessment but requires knowledge, application, and problem-solving abilities.

Yet many students do still come to the United States to pursue their college and graduate education. We are still a leader in the postsecondary institutions. However, as a university professor I am noticing that many (but certainly not all) of our United States students are less well prepared to enter college than the international students. (More about these issues in up-coming chapters.)

The educational problems we face in the United States are complex and at times seem staggering. The types of research needed to fully understand and solve our educational issues involve both quantitative and qualitative studies . . . one approach without the other will only give us part of the story.

As I began this important research project, I started by gathering archival information before outlining my methodology. The term "methodology" refers to the way in which we approach problems and seek answers (Taylor & Bogdan, 1998, p. 3). So I started by looking at the research and work of others dealing with educational distinction. (This process actually began many years ago, which culminated in the writing of *Hidden Dangers: Subtle Signs of Failing Schools* and has morphed into a much larger project of a global nature.)

It soon became clear to me that there was not one definition of educational excellence, nor was there any really hard and fast information. But all good researchers have to start somewhere. So I gathered what was available, defined my ideas as best I could at this early stage of emerging inquiry, and set about to devise a way to get firsthand information from talking with the people involved: students, teachers, parents, and administrators, as well as students and teachers from different countries.

I am not attempting to determine the causes of world problems, nor to cast blame on others. I am merely attempting to understand the social phenomenon regarding educational excellence from the teachers' and students' perspectives in the United States and in various countries around the world, for as Taylor and Bogdan (1998) assert: "The important reality is what people perceive it to be" (p. 3). So I chose a qualitative approach at this initial stage of investigation. (Quantitative studies will need to come later.)

Graziano and Raulin (2000) indicate that this type of research, utilizing surveys, questionnaires, or interview schedules is used effectively to obtain information from people in their natural settings. In this study, an unrestricted instrument was designed to allow individuals to respond with as much freedom as possible.

From this work I began to develop my questions; wondering what was preventing educational excellence in the United States and whether there were lessons to be learned from our global neighbors, wondering why some cultures value education so highly, pondering about the reasons some countries seem to excel in certain subjects, and so on.

We have much to gain from understanding the barriers preventing educational excellence in the United State and appreciating the successes that work educationally in other countries. Of course, we cannot assume that if something works well in one culture that it will in ours, but we have much to gain from the understanding of our global neighbors . . . indeed, without global knowledge we truly are not well educated.

I believe that it is important to understand the people, their values, their customs, and their unique situations from their perspectives. By experiencing their reality through their yes and voices, it is more readily possible to see patterns or themes and to develop insight and understanding into the workings of their world. Qualitative methodology allows this in-depth analysis, and the use of NVivo software was a welcomed assist in organizing and ascertaining emerging themes.

The identity of the respondents has been fully protected and will remain confidential. Any identifying information is purely coincidental since no specific case reflects any one respondent but is made up of composite sketches expressing the basic concerns.

The best way for me to get at the information I needed involved in-depth interviewing of students and teachers from the United States and around the globe. Such an approach allowed me to learn about events, activities, beliefs, and customs that I could not directly experience or observe. Not only was it impossible for me to travel to the far corners of the world, but I could not attend years and years of schooling in these various localities. I needed to depend upon the eyes, ears, and voices of those who had the experiences needed to answer my questions.

I coupled this research with my own previous observations and personal communications with students, teachers, parents, and administrators who have attended schooling within the United States. Although many of the conversations involved schools from the northeast section of the country, I have investigated other areas through an archival approach, and I suspect the information will ring true for many across the United States.

So I went about interviewing people who were willing to talk about their education, upbringing, and experiences, as students, parents, or educationally involved individuals in this country, and more recently with students and teachers who had grown up in different countries around the world. Some are college/university professors now, while others are from the younger generation and are still students, recently having come to the United States to continue their education.

Initially I had in mind vaguely formulated questions that were set forth in our interview schedule (Gunzelmann & van Loendersloot, 2007), but this was refined and revised as each interview yielded more information and themes began to emerge, which is often the case with qualitative analysis. This is an emerging analysis; one needs to stay open-minded and listen well to try and empathize with the person being interviewed to fully grasp the reality of that person's experiences. (See Appendix A, "Global Education Interview Guide and Questionnaire" from *Hidden Dangers: Subtle Signs of Failing Schools*.)

In some cases, more than one session was required in order to check out the understanding I had from the first session and to allow for more depth and discussion in the following session(s). Oftentimes, after taking time to reflect upon the first interview, either myself or the client would remember things that were important to the topics at hand.

In the actual interviews, it was important to have an open-ended line of questioning . . . or in some cases to just allow the subjects to "tell" their story. This was particularly the case when it was impossible to interview candidates due to constraints of distance. The face-to-face interviews had the advantage of time to develop rapport and a more natural give and take within the interview.

The focus of my studies was on understanding educational excellence from a broad perspective—worldwide practices, customs, beliefs, approaches, and settings that lead to excellence in learning. I also wanted to know the problems that children may face with getting an education.

So, then, the purpose of this study was:

1. To identify qualities in various settings that either hinder or lead to superior education.
2. To identify the qualities that are unique to healthy, educationally thriving environments.
3. To suggest how these healthy characteristics may be implemented in schools in the United States.
4. To get an idea of what education is like in other countries. Are there some countries that do a better job of addressing the educational needs of their people? Can these approaches be applied to other people and places? Can we learn from countries that are not thriving educationally? Can we learn from people and places where education is not available?

These questions make me realize that our world is such a cluttered place of information, facts, and theories. We need to sift through this information and synthesize what might be useful. Our culture is a noisy place, full of people expressing their thoughts, which requires listening differently while utilizing qualitative research to more fully understand, backed up by quantitative research to further substantiate the possibilities.

I was finally able to settle upon the following definition of "educational excellence." Thus, my description of an educated person involves the following:

> To be an educated person means to be more than just an intelligent person. To be educated we must be well learned, informed, aware, cultured, well grounded, civilized, prepared, and enlightened. (Webster's New World Thesaurus, 1990)

I will also add to this definition that an individual must be able to appreciate the differences of others, be able to think critically, have solid problem-solving skills, which requires creativity and innovation, and be able to work collaboratively to cope in our world.

I should note that others have also identified some of these critical elements as essential to the education of our children for the twenty-first century (Wagner, 2008). Clearly, there is no way of being well educated unless we are aware, enlightened, and well grounded with all aspects of our planet. It really does take not only a village, but a global understanding to obtain educational excellence!

An analysis of the current issues preventing excellence in the United States along with a broader, global perspective can free us from the constricting boundaries and unnecessary limits that currently hem us in and prevent us from reaching new heights academically and interpersonally. Even with the enormous technological advances our world has experienced, these unchallenged barriers still prevent excellence. As we learned in chapter 1, our current educational system is jam-packed with toxic boundaries and imbalances, all preventing us from reaching our fullest potential . . . and all are very unnecessary.

In Part II of *Barriers to Excellence* we will be doing just that: gaining awareness of the wide-ranging concerns involved while grasping the importance of expertise from many disciplines . . . most importantly, from our educators with a solid research-based foundation. We will see what has lead the United States down this slippery slope toward academic mediocrity . . . through an analysis of the boundary to excellence.

Note: My research team at Southern New Hampshire University, made up of undergraduate psychology students, has included over the past many years: *Ashley Bachelder, Noelle Bourgeois, Rachell Burrell, Russell Dudas, Ashley Gargano, Joshua Heyman, Heather Huntington, Angela Jackson, Lauren Lorenz, Andrea McMaster, Amanda Meenan, Lindsey Monti, Allysa Moriarty, Stacie Rivard, Nicole Sanborn, Lauren Twombly, and Tina van Loendersloot.*

Part II

The Barriers to Excellence

Chapter Four

Society and Culture

*First, Most Complex, and Most Controversial of the
Barriers to Excellence*

Living in the United States is wonderful. I love it here, as most U.S. citizens do. All countries have their own distinctive characteristics unique to their society; this is true in our culture as well. We are a culture that values individuality; we are a resourceful, tolerant, creative, and innovative nation, and a people who are very child centered in our approach to parenting and educating our young. All these are admirable qualities, yet some of these characteristics can become barriers, preventing us from attaining excellence, particularly when out of balance.

The word "balance" is of particular importance. Imbalance may prevent us from seeing the issues clearly. As we continue with our understanding of barriers to excellence, we will learn how many of these barriers are not negative traits in and of themselves. However, they become barriers when there is disequilibrium, an unwillingness to be flexible in one's thinking and to other possibilities that this becomes a barrier.

These admirable qualities can become toxic barriers rather than vibrant catalysts that they could be if in balance. Dr. Thomas Cottle (2001) expresses what I call cultural disequilibrium as the "ecology of peril".

CULTURAL DIFFERENCES

Clearly, the United States has many good values upon which this country was built . . . but I wonder if we are resting on our laurels a bit now. It seems some of these principles may have lost their powerful messages. Take, for example, the value of hard work. Our students often feel entitled; some say our students are disengaged, while others say our students are adrift, unmotivated, lazy, and irresponsible without a clue as to their purpose in life (Arum & Roksa, 2010).

Obviously, this description of our students is an exaggeration; many of our young people are outstanding students; responsible, community oriented, focused, and motivated. Yet there may be a grain of truth to the portrayal for many . . . and this needs to change.

THE WORK ETHIC

In the early history of the United States, hard work was equated with a virtuous life, and in many ways, one's survival depended upon one's hard work in the fields, at one's job, and in one's home in order to provide for the family members. This work belief stemmed from the Protestant work ethic . . . hard work was seen as a virtue.

Somewhere along the line, as we became more prosperous, the need to work hard was slowly replaced with the desire to relax and enjoy life. But what is misconstrued is the idea that one can fully enjoy life when one is not living up to one's potential, discovering and preparing for one's unique purpose in our world. Here again, we have constructed a barrier to excellence in need of balance.

At times it appears our values of society seem to be turned upside down. We used to have a strong work ethic and took pride in doing good work. What changed? As the good life became more possible and we were able to relax . . . why did we go the route of laziness? Like a drugged "culture," there seems to be a disconnect of not feeling the self-dissatisfaction of doing poor work. Often students turn off in the classroom, almost daring a teacher to try and spoon-feed them the curriculum.

Many kids in the United States seem to believe that there is always time to learn information at a later date; it's not seen as cool to work one's hardest. For example, in the United States, education is seen as a right . . . and in many ways is taken for granted. In the United States, students are required to go to school through age sixteen in most states, but the attitude in the culture is not one that really values education. Oh, lip service is given to the value of a good education . . . but many do not see the connection between a good education and the need to work hard in order to get that education.

Education is not something that can be given . . . it is something that must be earned through hard work, experience, and desire to obtain it. This reminds me of a quotation from one of the global research interviews from Japan. Reiko said, "In Japan hard work is a beauty" (personal communication, 2008). This statement really caught my attention and pointed out the difference between many students in the United States and many from other countries around the world where students would not have high self-esteem if they believed they were not doing their best work.

SOCIETAL VIEW ON INDIVIDUAL DIFFERENCES

So let us take a look at another core value. To live in the United States means we value our individuality, our uniqueness . . . or do we? Well, it seems we do value our individuality to a point . . . we value our freedom of speech and our other individual rights and privileges. However, on the other hand, we seem to become a nation that does not tolerate differences well.

We do not appreciate the uniqueness of others as much as we might think. There seems to be a need to label or diagnose everyone rather than seeing the positive aspects in some differences. We diagnose children with attention problems (being overly attentive or underattentive); we diagnose children with intense interests in a subject; and we diagnose children who may have exceptional hearing or sensitivity in some areas.

Please do not get me wrong . . . some of these children do indeed have problems that need both medical and educational interventions . . . but frequently children are labeled because they may not be thriving in a situation due to other circumstances. (These were discussed in-depth in *Hidden Dangers: Subtle Signs of Failing Schools*.)

Children who are labeled, or in many cases misdiagnosed, are often viewed differently by their peers, teachers, and most unfortunately by their parents. These children are thus deprived of being fully understood and sabotaged from attaining their fullest potential. Instead, their potential gets crushed by the very labels that are supposed to help them.

According to research by Paine and Schleicher (2011), it is interesting to note that several of the countries thriving academically do not recognize disorders in the same manner that we do here in the United States. At the very least, each child is seen as having the potential to achieve at a high level, and it is necessary that they do so. The expectations are maintained at a high level.

Hopefully the reader can see the need for balance here. High expectations are necessary for excellence in education. The problem comes when we err too far one way or the other, lowering expectations so that children are not frustrated and depressed by their limitations or raising them so high that children become frustrated and anxious. For the most part, we do not need labels to balance the educational programs for children in our schools. The diagnoses belong in the hands of the medical doctors when specific disorders requiring specific interventions are needed.

Unfortunately, the more common scenario for children who are labeled is that they are misunderstood and/or impeded by the label of just being different or not meeting the cultural stereotype of being strong, fit, and athletic. Elaine Aron (1996), in her research on the sensitive person, believes that in the United States there is a negative bias toward these individuals.

The cultural bias mislabels these individuals, totally missing the essence of the trait with all its positive aspects. It appears that the trait of being sensitive, which she explains, characterizes people who are more careful, deeper processors of information. She also believes that people with this trait are more conscientious, cautious, and wise people (p. 7).

I tend to concur with Aron's work and the inherent outcome that our cultural partiality can indeed set up a barrier to excellence. She rightly points out that in many cultures, including Japan, Sweden, and China, the Japanese psychologists and researchers seem to expect the highly sensitive individuals to perform better. (Note that these countries are all at the top of the list of educational achievement!)

The negative inclination toward the sensitive individuals comes through loud and clear when looking at the classic work of Margaret Mead. She explains that in every culture there is really only one ideal . . . and this ideal type makes up only a narrow few of the population. Yet this ideal persona is interwoven in "every thread of the social fabric—in the care of the young child, the games the children play, the songs the children sing, the political organization, the religious observance, the art and the philosophy" (Aron, 1996, p. 15).

Here in the United States, this ideal may be typed as a strong, good-looking, athletic type who does reasonably well in school . . . but not the supersmart geek. One can see how children may yearn to become and even idolize this popular stereotype rather than valuing their uniqueness, their gifts, and their individuality.

In contrast, Aron points out: "In China 'shy' and 'sensitive' children were among those most chosen by others to be friends or playmates. (In Mandarin, the word for shy or quiet means good or well-behaved; sensitive can be translated as 'having understanding,' a term of praise.)" (Aron, 1996, p. 15).

Such a barrier as narrow-mindedness to differences, or at the very least not celebrating and valuing our uniqueness, is definitely out of balance and can in turn set up new barriers to excellence involving inequities of race, gender, socioeconomic advantage, religion, age, or any other grouping . . . all limiting potential toward excellence.

MISGUIDED CULTURAL IDOLS

One can easily see how this theory lends itself to our out-of-balance idolization of misguided cultural icons or maybe, more accurately, overly valued cultural icons, at the expense of the more important cultural needs. Now do not take this the wrong way, but our societal viewpoint on our valued icons is really convoluted. There is nothing wrong with our national pastimes of baseball and football, our athletes, or our movie or rock stars. These people all contribute in their own way to our society and to enjoyment of our leisure time. Their work is demanding, and they are well recognized for their efforts.

My concern is why these individuals are idolized in our country, paid extremely high salaries . . . while our teachers, researchers, and the like are paid such low salaries, often requiring them to work two and three jobs . . . while they are trying to do one of the most vitally important jobs to the longevity of our country, that is, educating our youth! The apparently low status of education in our country is directly opposed to the lip service we give to this central cultural value. Our behavior speaks louder than our words.

THE VALUE OF EDUCATION IN THE UNITED STATES

Modern cynics and skeptics . . . see no harm in paying those to whom they entrust the minds of their children a smaller wage than is paid to those to whom they entrust the care of their plumbing.
—John F. Kennedy

To better understand the lower level of importance placed on education in our country, all one need really do is look to our cultural icons. Who are our local heroes; who do our young people look up to; who is paid the most money? Certainly it is not our teachers or our scholars who are held in such high esteem . . . although we may give lip service to this ideal.

In the United States this is more a thought than a reality. We often hear an alarming statement, "Those who can't . . . teach." In other words, those who have not been as successful in school and cannot get accepted to the competitive colleges go into teaching! Naturally, this is not the case with most of our dedicated teachers, but it does reflect a very serious cultural value . . . or, rather, lack of value for education.

Indeed, this too can be seen as an issue of respect and necessity: those who can do so go into more lucrative lines of work. But the good teachers are paid so poorly that they often need to work second jobs to make ends meet. This does not make sense, for then they cannot be available to their students as they need to be when committed, truly devoted to their reason for being— teaching. Our global voices from many other countries around the world paint a very different picture.

Teachers are held in the highest esteem . . . in some cases, even higher than doctors and lawyers. Many of the highest achieving students are selected to become teachers and are well supported by their government to do so, including being given tuition for teacher education and training. This is indeed the case in world leading Finland as articulated by Pasi Sahlberg, (2010).

Respect for parents was very important in India as well . . . may be even more so than for teachers. "Every family member asks how you are doing at school, what subjects are your favorite, etc. Education is highly valued" (personal communication). Yet we also know that, at least intellectually, U.S. parents realize that it is important for their children to be well educated if they are to get into college, get a good job, and succeed in life . . . to obtain the American dream.

Actually however, there is much more at stake than jobs and dreams. If our children continue on this current educational downward spiral, they will not be competitive with others from around the world. The United States will no longer be seen as a significant and knowledgeable influence in the world authorities.

Have we become a lost culture; void of identity and purpose . . . of a reason to strive for goals, to better ourselves, and to help others? Since the 1970s there has been a strong push toward trying to fill the empty voids by buying more than we need, and we have seen the devastation this can cause with our economy and people losing their homes and life savings. Have we become a culture that defines itself by what we have rather than what we do? Rather than by purposeful, educated reason for contributing in a positive way to our society?

STRONG SENSE OF ETHICS AND MORAL REASONING

The United States has a strong foundation built upon strong ethics and moral reasoning. I fear this too may be out of balance and eating away at the very core foundational beliefs within our society. Honesty and hard work were always essential; valuing individual rights and differences, trying our best, and striving for excellence helped to guide the United States into a world leader based upon humanitarian principles of caring, sharing, and prospering. Let us not lose sight of these core principles. Let us not continue to allow these founding values to be out of balance, creating barriers to educational excellence for our children and for our country.

The United States really needs a wake-up call . . . for our cultural values are fading, and they are impacting the education of our students and ultimately impacting our nation. Wake up, America . . . we are in trouble!

COMPETITION RUN AMUCK

We are a competitive people, no doubt about that fact. This too has both its positive and negative sides. However, it too is out of balance. It is always nice to be in first place when playing any game, but the education of our children is not a game, and winning the "educational Olympics" is the wrong focus. The important issue at hand is to attain educational excellence . . . not winning. Having our students well educated, able to contribute to society in meaningful ways, and upholding our high principles . . . this is what is important.

Putting too much emphasis on accountability and testing shows this out of balance problem and unfortunately assures failure. Yes, our schools and our children need to be accountable, but we have yet to find an adequate, fair way of demonstrating accountability. Using student test scores to demonstrate teacher's responsibility is fraught with problems. The tests used were not designed for these purposes and are quite fallible. It is really an unethical, unreliable, and invalid use of testing, which will further imbalance the equity problems in our educational system.

Additionally, as for the overuse of tests, with students trying to obtain excellence . . . that is statistically a losing battle since half of all students must be below the norm. I'm not saying we should get rid of testing . . . but tests do need to be use judiciously and wisely. Readers interested in more information on this subject should read Deborah Meier's (2002) *In Schools We Trust* and Alfie Kohn's (1992) *No Contest*.

Our schools are caught up in a testing obsession that has its roots in the accountability movement of earlier decades. Don't get me wrong—being accountable is a good thing, and student learning should be measured and documented, but how we are determining a student's learning is the problem. We're putting too much confidence in tests, and the scores are interpreted as an accurate reflection of a student's knowledge, skills, and abilities. Many students do not perform well on certain types of tests.

Testing in and of itself is a neutral process; it is when testing is misused that it can become a dangerous process. I have been involved with assessing students' learning for many years now. Earlier in my career, I was involved in diagnosing students with learning disabilities and other disorders.

After years of using tests to measure, diagnose, and establish appropriate educational plans, I have done a 180-degree turn in my viewpoint on the usefulness and effectiveness of many traditional tests. In fact, I see many assessment approaches as being imprecise and even damaging for many students.

The essential questions we must be asking on educational assessment approaches include

- Are individual differences respected?
- Do the policies encourage teaching to the test?
- Does the assessment approach fit our culture?
- Does the approach validly measure our curriculum? And does it do so reliably?
- Are we overlooking more essential learning, reflection, creativity, problem-solving abilities?

Bottom line: Are our students prepared for college, work and life? Are they successful?

CHANGE . . . BUT RESEARCH BASED

Yes, we are a country that values change . . . but sometimes we change too readily and throw the baby out with the bathwater. Change is a good thing as well, but it has become a barrier to excellence when change in the educational areas is not based upon solid research or is implemented based upon misinterpretation of research, is implemented because of money issues, a matter of convenience, political ramifications, and so on. Change is good when it is done for the right reasons and done well.

TIME AND IMPATIENCE

Time also has important cultural implications. We are a people who can act when necessary, and we can get a job done well, but we are often seen as a nation in a hurry. We live in a fast-paced society, full of opportunity, but there is a shadow side to this intensity. We hurry our children to grow up too quickly, overscheduling their days; we teach concepts to children earlier, without a solid foundation, allowing for little family time and play, which is so essential to learning.

There is no doubt that hurrying is a detriment to excellence. For example, if we do not take the necessary time to research and implement educational strategies well, or if we do not give students time to reflect upon their studies to achieve deeper learning, or if we do not look back in time to understand our mistakes and prevent future problems, our quickness is a barrier.

Along these same lines, one of my advanced research students commented on "the instantaneous nature of our society, fueled by technology, which has drastically altered our culture and the way we approach everyday life." The research student goes on to state:

> Nicholas Carr wrote an article in 2008 called "Is Google Making Us Stupid?" In it he talked about how the Internet is changing the way we think and interpret information. More and more people read the news online, and these stories are becoming shorter and shorter as people have less time to read them. This consolidates the information, making it simpler and easier to digest, but also less in depth and less abstract.

As Heyman (2011) further hypothesizes, it also makes the information shorter, which over time lowers our attention span. If we're used to reading a three- or four-paragraph story and end up getting one twice as long, chances are that halfway through we'll start retaining less and less information, because we are now not accustomed to reading that much.

THE CHANGING FAMILY

The family structure also has changed in the United States over the last fifty-plus years too, creating barriers to excellence. Today's families are often headed by single parents struggling to make ends meet, parents working two and three jobs with little or no extended family to assist, all taking away from the essential time for parenting. Most parents want the best for their children but have little time or energy left over.

Of course, there are many more serious family issues as well: domestic violence, abuse, alcohol and drug dependence, neglect, unemployment, homelessness, and so on. Academic excellence will be difficult to attain without addressing these issues as well.

INFORMALITY AND MISPERCEIVED ARROGANCE

Some even say that we are a less formal culture than many and that it is "un-American to show arrogance or superiority." (University of Wisconsin–Madison International Student Service, 2010). Yes, this too is true . . . but sometimes we may be forgetting this core value when we believe that we are the world leaders in education . . . clearly we are not.

Likewise when we believe that others should all learn English and there is no need for our students to learn different languages, or that others should learn of our culture but we know little of their history, geography, or culture. Indeed this is a barrier: the flip side of this virtue unfortunately could be perceived as arrogance or superiority, an attitude that is not how we want to see ourselves and that clearly impedes educational excellence.

INDIVIDUALISM AND LEARNING IN ISOLATION

This brings us to the barrier of learning in isolation, which is a theme that emerged from my research and which one of my research students expanded on (Heyman, 2011). Americans by nature seem to be individualistic and have a can-do attitude. Yes, we are bright, capable, and resourceful people, used to taking care of matters for ourselves.

But academic distinction requires both an individualistic approach and collaboration. Naturally, this requires that we not believe we can learn everything in isolation from others. Being truly educated includes knowledge, understanding, and skills from a global/shared perspective. It seems we are out of balance with this issue, creating yet another barrier to excellence.

Many of our traits can work in our favor to break down these barriers and rebalance our system . . . and there are many who can and will help us to do this. We are a practical, optimistic, and determined society and believe that change can be a good thing . . . and it can be, as we shall see in part III of *Barriers to Excellence.*

In the meantime, there is much more depth needed to our understanding of how these out-of-balance barriers have impacted our students, our teachers, our attainment of educational excellence. In chapter 5, the political barriers preventing excellence are examined.

Chapter Five

Political Barriers to Excellence

Multifaceted and Difficult, but Not Impossible to Resolve

Our government is really quite remarkable and works well most of the time. However, when it comes to educating our youth we are losing ground and stumbling over needless barriers. The government's role in education is to ensure research-based policies are well developed, ably applied, continually revised and updated when needed, and available to all children equally. Government funding for the education of our children should be a top priority, not the budget item that gets slashed when the economic picture is challenging.

According to the Democracy at Risk Report (Forum for Education and Democracy, 2008), the United States has one of the most inequitably funded education systems of all industrialized nations (pp. 21–22). Additionally, we have lost much of the educational gains made by African American and Hispanic students during the 1970s (Forum, 2008, p. iv).

As a nation, our children drop out at alarming rates, and of those who stay, we are seeing that they are less able to compete with their global peers (PISA, 2006; Paine & Schleicher, 2011). Our system has failed these individuals, and we have lost tremendous potential.

The news is no better in 2011 than it was a few years ago; we continue to inequitably fund schools, lose our skilled teachers to other better-paying professions, hire inexperienced and/or untrained teachers in our most difficult schools, and overuse and misuse standardized tests, creating barriers to education that are difficult for even the most skilled and experienced teachers to overcome. Linda Darling-Hammond (2011) is quite succinct on this point when she says:

It is not acceptable to have schools in our cities and poor rural districts staffed by a revolving door of beginning and often untrained teachers, many of whom see this as charity work they do on the way to a real job. And it is not acceptable that the major emphasis of educational reform is on bubbling in the Scranton test booklets, the results of which will be used to rank and sort schools and teachers, so that those at the bottom can be fired or closed. (Darling-Hammond, 2011)

It is very difficult to ferret out the political issues from the societal issues impacting education in our country since in reality they are really interwoven. However, it is important to study these as separate entities in order to more fully grasp the complexity involved. Political policies are not as straightforward as the politicians would like us to believe . . . even when they are being sincere. Because politics are political, thus biased in nature, there are a number of ways that affairs of state can become barriers.

POLITICAL BARRIER NUMBER ONE: THE NATURE OF POLITICS

In order to overcome the political barriers we first need to identify them and then be able to cut through the political red tape that slows down implementation of needed changes . . . or waters them down so much that the changes bear little resemblance to the original identified need. Thus, the first political barrier involves *the essence of politics* itself. Our party system works well in many instances . . . but sometimes it can impede needed changes due to the politicking and posturing of each party's side. (This barrier involves societal, bureaucratic walls.)

The American people have seen this dance of politics so many times before that we have grown weary of the process. Our two-party system does often provide a great check-and-balance system for our government, but it can sometimes be a barrier when, for political reasons, we cannot seem to do what is best for our children and ultimately for our country.

We have seen this with the economic issues, and we are likely to see much more of this irresponsible, short-sighted behavior. Bottom line: our representatives and senators really need to stop playing games with our children's and our country's future. Just do what is right, what is needed, in a timely manner, without all the grandstanding, and using a sustainable approach for our future.

Even with the political vision of our current leaders, President Obama and Secretary of Education Arne Duncan, we seem to have reverted to more of the same old policies that just are not working. No doubt the United States has had much to handle over the last several years, including inherited and needless wars, threats of terrorism, economic crises, and numerous natural disasters . . . but the education of our children should be our highest priority once safety is established. Education is really the answer to solving (for the long term) many of our country's and the world's problems.

Thus there is a critical need for us all to be on the same page—to work toward educational reform—not fighting with one another for political posturing. We need a leader with vision, political force, and finesse. Currently we do have a political leader with the vision but without the knowledge of the cutting-edge research from various disciplines. President Obama . . . listen to the teachers, to the parents, and to the children; listen to the researchers, the psychologists, the pediatricians, and those in direct contact with and who care for our children.

POLITICAL BARRIER NUMBER TWO: FAIR AND EQUITABLE FUNDING—A NATIONAL PRIORITY

Plain and simple, we need a better way to fund our schools and meet the needs of our children. An approach that is both just and unbiased is essential. At both the federal and state levels, education must be a funding high priority that does not become superseded by other needs in a tight economy.

There is something rather inappropriate with many states' approach to raising money for schools through lotteries. Not only does this reinforce the gambling addictions of many, but it seems to leave the education of our children to chance, as if it were not an important enough issue to be a more integral part of governments' budgets . . . nor does it alleviate the inequity of funding among our schools.

There is an alarming phenomenon called the "school-to-prison pipeline" that reportedly is in large part due to the inequity within our society (Forum, 2008, pp. 21–22).

Currently we have the most costly prison system in the world with one of the largest populations of inmates, mostly made up of high-school dropouts. According to Darling-Hammond (2011) it now costs us forty thousand dollars per year to house the inmates rather than the ten thousand dollars per year it would have cost for adequate education of these individuals. All this money being spent on the prisons could be earmarked for education. It seems as if we have even lost more ground in this area since 2008.

Darling-Hammond refers to these problems as

> the aggressive neglect of our children. With 1 out of 4 living poverty—far more than any other industrialized country (nearly double what it was 30 years ago); a more tattered safety net—more who are homeless, without public health care, and without food security; a more segregated and inequitable system of public education, in which the top schools spend 10 times more than

the lowest spending; we nonetheless have a defense budget larger than that of the next 20 countries combined and greater disparities in wealth than any leading country. (Darling-Hammond, 2011)

Making educational opportunities available and equitable includes assuring that essential needs are met for safety, healthy buildings, and nutritious meals along with superior educators, equipment, and materials, as we will see in the upcoming chapters. Also, meeting early needs of children is a prerequisite for optimal learning and includes health care, quality child care, and parenting programs. Our government must support and ensure that these basic needs are met.

POLITICAL BARRIER NUMBER THREE: NO TEAM APPROACH

Clearly, the third political barrier involves *the lack of a centralized input for researchers from interdisciplinary fields as well as the synthesis of the findings, monitoring of implementation, and revisions as needed.* (This barrier involves bureaucratic and procedural problems.) Saving this faltering educational system requires an interdisciplinary approach from those involved with children and learning; not from the businessmen or the lawyers who are not experts on the needs of the children. And the needs run deep in this country.

The basic needs of children must be addressed to set the stage for optimal learning. These include medical and dental care, early childhood interventions, parenting support, healthy nutrition, and regular exercise and well-run after-school programs. It is remarkable to note that other academically thriving countries do support their children in this manner.

According to Darling-Hammond, both Singapore and Canada are meeting the children's needs: "They ensure that all children have housing, health care, and food security. They fund their schools equitably. They invest in the highest-quality preparation, mentoring and professional development for school leaders, completely at government expense" (Darling-Hammond, 2011).

Such a team approach needs to be well organized and synergistic, and team members must communicate with one another effectively. The educational excellence team should be able to rise above the political tendency to want to take credit for successes and pass the buck when results are disappointing. The team's mission is to systematically figure out what works in specific situations and to implement the research-based strategies successfully and reliably.

Without full knowledge from the interdisciplinary team, our political leaders are more apt to buckle under pressure to do much of the same that has not been working . . . or to again implement policies that are ineffective, putting too much reliance upon current forms of assessment, which are not valid or reliable with all students, and fail to support the necessary changes required to build and sustain the educational excellence of our students.

Additionally, all of the educationally thriving countries do have a centralized educational organization, or ministry of education as it is called in many other areas of the world, like the U.S. Department of Education. Standards are set by such centralized branches of government but are well funded and well researched, with excellent follow-through, as well as being flexible and equitable in nature.

POLITICAL BARRIER NUMBER FOUR: POLITICAL ISSUES AT THE STATE AND LOCAL LEVELS

This brings us to the fourth political barrier: *the poor communication and response between federal, state, and local branches of government.* This barrier involves bureaucratic, procedural, and practical barriers.

It seems as if the U.S Department of Education does not know what the state DOEs are dealing with, and likewise it seems as if the state DOEs are out of touch with the issues that school personnel must actually deal with in their local communities and schools. Instead, the departments of education at both the state and federal levels are seen as rather ineffective yet punitive arms of the government that further complicate the already difficult jobs our teachers and administrators are trying to cope with on a daily basis.

Our SNHU research team on global education has found that all thriving countries have a central ministry of education, but the approaches of these centralized government operations are to solve the problems . . . not to penalize schools and teachers. Instead, it appears these ministries have faith in their teachers and administrators to implement policies well and to adapt the educational plans to their particular situations.

They trust in their teachers because they chose the cream-of-the-crop students and encouraged them to become teachers; they support their teachers educationally and financially and hold them in high esteem. Furthermore, these ministries understand that a one-size-fits-all approach for all schools is really not feasible.

Such an open, flexible, supportive attitude would work well in our culture too, that is, if we do not punish and reinforce the tendency for our educators to be defensive, in debt, and in fear of their jobs. Our departments of education face a monumental task in improving our schools. It is quite difficult for anyone in this position to not become defensive in attitude and approach and to want to find the quick fix for our faltering schools. But defensiveness and impulsiveness have no place here (Summit, 2011).

We need leaders in government and in our departments of education, both at the national and state levels, who grasp the unique problems within our society and who grasp the unique problems within their jurisdiction, their states and local communities. Their intent must be to decipher the problems . . . not to punish schools that are struggling, but to support and to solve these issues.

To do so we must have individuals in these key positions who are well educated in research and open to research from related interdisciplinary fields, who understand the fallibility of assessment, who use tests for the right reasons, and most importantly, who have the ability to see how our schools can be different and not repeat the same problems that they have experienced as products of our long-struggling educational system.

POLITICAL BARRIER NUMBER FIVE: LEARNING IN ISOLATION

This political barrier involves cultural, psychological, and cognitive issues. Certainly there have been times in history when we needed to step back and lick our wounds, time to recover, just as all people do after tragedies, deaths, and any number of possible losses. Our country is currently suffering from an educational loss, and we need time to get back our footing, to find our way. But the way back, indeed the way to educational excellence can be found by reaching out beyond ourselves . . . to the interdisciplinary fields as discussed, as well as to our global educational thrivers.

The United States prides itself on having a global awareness and respect for our neighbors. I believe this is true . . . to a point. Yes, we are interested in the well-being of all global citizens and will help those in need when possible. And yes, we understand full well that we have much to learn from other cultures and that we all must work together on solving world problems such as global warming, pandemics, and the like.

Many Americans, although they may not admit it, and possibly may not even be aware of it, deep down inside think that our way is the right way, and thus our pride and stubbornness may get in our way of seeking solutions outside of ourselves. Our strong sense of independence needs to be balanced with a strong understanding of the need and healthy approach of interdependence at times.

Naturally, we know that this is not always the case. What may be right in one culture may be wrong in another . . . and usually if we take the time to learn about others, we can understand their points of view. However, we have much to learn from our studies on global education.

Globally thriving countries all have standards-based instruction as we are trying to implement here. The difference is that so many of those involved in U.S. education are naysayers. They don't believe that standards are necessary . . . but indeed, research has born out that the thriving countries all have a standards-based curriculum. However, we do not want to use the standards to penalize, label, or otherwise impede learning . . . as they have been used to date.

In the academically flourishing countries, the standards work because those countries believe in them, implement them well, conduct follow-up studies, and tweak their instructional approaches when needed. Bottom line: they solve their educational challenges.

Yet speaking of standards, we need to look at curriculum issues even within this chapter on politics . . . because standards will be developed on national and state levels. Our current expectations are quite limiting and putting our students at a disadvantage in our global economy.

Our educational expectations need to be much broader. For our learning to be excellent, it needs to be as full and as complete as possible. We must have access to global expertise in order to understand, to experience, and to come to a higher level of appreciation of learning. We have much to gain from embracing the concepts of a complete education.

Yet so often we are isolated in our learning with barriers put before us. You can see it even in our curriculum. For example, very few of our students in the United States become fluent in a foreign language. Partly this is because of the manner in which languages are taught and when they are introduced in the curriculum (more about this later), but in part it is because of a belief that English is the world language, which others should learn to speak as we do.

Well, others can speak English, and many speak other languages as well! In all countries in which my global education research team has interviewed, all students are taking foreign languages at early ages and throughout their school years. Many become fluent in two, three, or even more languages. We are definitely at a disadvantage here.

My global education researchers have seen a similar pattern developing with the scope and depth of how subjects are taught, including geography, history, mathematics, and even physical education. We are trailing sadly behind because of our obliviousness to the current academic needs. The world has changed and so have the needs of our students.

Not knowing is not understanding. Not understanding is ignorance. Ignorance creates barriers . . . ignorance of other cultures creates bigotry and potentially even wars. Certainly this is not good for our foreign policy, but it is also bad for the economy. Actually, it just seems un-American, for the United States is not made up of any one nationality . . . but of many. By understanding all cultures, people, and languages we can make rational decisions based upon what is in the best interests of all people within our own country and the people of the world.

It should be clear that political barriers need to be understood both on the nationwide and on the state and local levels. The political problems we are seeing in Indiana, Ohio, and Wisconsin over teachers' unions will likely crop up in others states as well, given the economic situation of many states that find themselves at the door of bankruptcy.

But unions are not necessarily the problem . . . although clearly the unions need to work cooperatively with our government and vice versa. The collective bargaining process is deeply ingrained in the history and culture of the United States and in fact is a required subject as part of the curriculum in U.S. history.

We are beginning to see some change in this area. In March 2011, the International Summit on the Teaching Profession brought together education ministers, national union leaders, education organization leaders, and accomplished teachers from high-performing countries in order to identify best practices, and it was clear that the unions were working cooperatively and successfully with those involved.

We also learned from this March 2011 international summit that the highest-performing country, Singapore, puts its best teachers in the most challenging schools and classrooms (U.S. Department of Education, 2011). We need such a policy in our country, but teachers must be well compensated and supported to bring all students to their potential level of excellence, and each teacher must see this opportunity as a professional challenge to demonstrate excellence as well.

Yes, we need to groom our brightest to become teachers; yes, we need to update and improve teacher education and the continuing education of teachers; and yes, teachers need to be knowledgeable about psychometrics and research methodology, skilled in conducting and interpreting both qualitative and quantitative approaches and then implementing them appropriately, adapting to their particular classes and individual students. This is a task for a superstar, for our teachers need to be of the highest caliber, with superior education, training, and support if we are to attain educational excellence.

POLITICAL BARRIER NUMBER SIX: IT IS NOT A RACE . . . IT IS NOT THE EDUCATIONAL OLYMPICS

By nature we are a competitive people, as we have seen in chapter 4 . . . but this out-of-balance cultural trait impacts our educational policies and political platforms in an unhelpful manner. If our politicians develop policies that are geared toward the end goal of winning the educational Olympics, we are set up to fail . . . and this is partly what is wrong with previous policies such as No Child Left Behind and numerous others since the 1980s and the subsequent decline.

Our government policies on education must be solidly research based and include both qualitative and quantitative research methodologies. Research on global education is beginning to reveal why many U.S. students are lagging behind their counterparts in other countries. Most of those countries' curricula, teaching approaches, and teacher-preparation programs are based upon research and are equally available to all children. Their resources, both in school and out of school, are strongly supported by government funding.

A good research example that should be heeded by our government policies comes from the neuropsychological expert Jill Stamm (2007), who clearly illustrates that learning begins much earlier than formal education. The implication is not to abandon the trend toward earlier formal schooling; rather, *parents must be provided with parenting skills programs and well-run day care and preschool programs*. Government funding is an essential component of such programs.

Many parents are not allowed adequate time or don't have the necessary knowledge or skills to provide such conditions. Our government must fund and assist with the development of well-researched early intervention programs for all children to begin to equalize the educational opportunities for all children.

Other foundational needs include early and sustainable programs to develop safe, healthy home and learning environments, healthy food, access to excellent health care, and the availability of stimulating, balanced afterschool care for the children of working parents so that the essential early needs of our children are supported, paving the way for optimal learning.

One key to the success of other higher-performing nations has been the provision of the *out-of-school learning supports*, including child care, free, nutritious lunches, safe buildings, superior teachers, and educational supportive interventions, along with health and dental care (Forum, 2008, p. vi). Ideally, well-funded, solid-research-based early intervention programs would begin to equalize educational opportunities for all U.S.children.

Safe and healthy schools are critical to learning through all the growing years . . . not just the early ages. Our children deserve to learn in healthy environments free from toxins and in buildings meeting safety codes. Wholesome, nutritious foods served for lunches and snacks must become the rule to support the healthy development of the children, allowing for optimal learning. *Government-funded programs* can help make this a reality.

Increased support for technology can also help make education more equitable. Thanks to advances in technology, even inner-city and remote rural classrooms can directly access content experts and premier teachers.

Furthermore, accessing such expertise will raise the bar of excellence for all teachers. However, teachers need specific training in the use of the new technologies and how to apply them well in learning situations.

Government policies on assessment and testing must be helpful. The No Child Left Behind Act may have at first appeared helpful, but ultimately it caused schools to concern themselves more with scores than with student needs (Forum, 2008, p. 25). By overemphasizing an unreliable measure of performance, such mandates reduce student interest and teacher passion (Gunzelmann, 2004, 2005, 2011a).

We must not put too much emphasis on any one test (including the PISA assessments). I am in full agreement with Sternberg (2011), who points out the narrowness of many assessments. It is not that we should rule out these instruments, but we should add broader assessments to include portfolio and performance assessments. The chapter on testing addresses these issues in more depth.

Let's put this in perspective as to how much is really needed to revise the educational issues currently experienced in the United States. I was alarmed when I saw the statistics regarding the monetary needs of the schools in the United States. According to the *Democracy at Risk* report (Forum, 2008), the United States could totally revise the current educational disaster with an investment cost about the same as one month of our involvement in Iraq!

Additionally, by improving education for all students, we will be *decreasing costs* through lost wages and lost taxes from dropouts and through less need for remediation programs, as well as the millions needed for the prison population in part due to inadequate and unequal education (Forum, 2008).

Government can and must play an important role in the education of the children. Doing what is best for children means trusting and relying on professionals in the related fields of education, psychology, neuroscience, and medicine; doing what is best, not what is cheapest; doing what works, not more of the same old approaches that have intensified educational decline; and developing policies that are sustainable in order to maintain excellence in the education of our youth.

There is no time like the present. Our current administration in Washington can make these changes to bring about educational excellence for all children if we all work together.

Chapter Six

Economic Barriers to Excellence

It should be clear to the reader by now how complex and interrelated these barriers have become to our educational system. The economic barriers to excellence have specific economic issues, but all are related to society, culture and political issues as well as the barriers to be explored in the upcoming chapters. Currently we are facing a worldwide economic crisis; one that has multiple causes and thus far, no simple or quick fixes. So, too, it is with the educational predicament we face.

Yes, we need to be careful with how our money is spent, but certainly there is no more important need than the educational excellence of our children. Today's youth must be well prepared for competing in the world job market and ultimately with assisting to bring about long-term economic growth and stability. All changes take time, but we cannot afford to make further mistakes with the education of our children. Economically this will cost money, and it is essential that it become a top priority for our nation.

Here it seems there are too many naysayers regarding the education budgets in the United States. Education budgets seem to get reduced whenever another group needs funding. Bottom line: the money is essential in order to obtain educational excellence. We need to put our money where our mouths are and earmark the necessary funding for the education of our youth.

I am aware that many of our citizens are currently unemployed, losing their homes, and requiring assistance. I am a firm believer in helping those in need, supporting the elderly, making sure all U.S. citizens have health and dental care and that they are contributing to our society in a manner in which they are capable. We have a social responsibility to assist in times of need, yet on the other hand, no one should be allowed to take advantage of the system.

Clearly we have an economic barrier here in need of balancing, with our society's values as we saw in chapter 4 and the entitlement that it seems so many feel. Paradoxically, our educational decline may involve our *prosperity* and many youths' *attitude of entitlement* without the understanding of the need to work to obtain their goals.

THE PRICE OF PROSPERITY

One might think that more money will solve all of our educational woes. Certainly more money can help some of the problems, such as making education equally available to all students, including educational opportunities, access to excellent teachers, and availability of technology and supplies. But in countries where money is more prevalent there may indeed be other problems that develop within the culture that erode the importance of a good education.

For example, in the United States education is seen as a right and in many ways is taken for granted. U.S. students are required to go to school through age sixteen in most states, but the attitude in the culture is not one that really values education. Oh, lip service is given to the value of a good education . . . but most do not see the connection between a good education and the need to work hard in order to get that education.

Education is not something that can be given . . . it is something that must be earned through hard work, experience, and desire to obtain it. There is a tremendous waste of talent, intelligence, and potential with unmotivated students.

As we learned in chapter 4 in the early years of the United States, hard work was equated with a virtuous life, and in many ways one's survival depended upon one's hard work in the fields, at one's job, and in one's home in order to provide for the family members. This work belief stemmed from the Protestant work ethic . . . hard work was seen as a virtue.

Somewhere along the line as we became more prosperous economically, the need to work hard was slowly replaced with the desire to relax and enjoy life. But what is misconstrued is the idea that one can fully enjoy life when one is not living up to one's potential, discovering and preparing for one's unique purpose in our world. Monetary loss, personal loss, and ultimately potential global loss is the result.

Often students turn off in the classroom, almost daring a teacher to try and spoon-feed them the curriculum. Kids in the United States seem to believe that there is always time to learn information later. It's not seen as "cool" to work ones' hardest, particularly when one does not need to. In some ways this is in stark contrast to a value from Asian countries, where one does not want to be number one because then there is nothing to work toward. But to be in second place makes one want to strive harder toward the goal of being first (personal communication, 2008 Japan interview).

It seems that in all developed countries around the world education is provided free to all children (or almost free in some cases). Governments approve the curriculum and regulate the schools in all aspects: what is taught, how it is taught, assessment approaches, length of schooling, and so on, although in some countries education is not equal because students do not have access . . . particularly those living in poverty and in remote villages too far away to be able to access schools or teachers.

Yet it is interesting to note that many such children seem to value education very dearly. In some ways the issues of prosperity, or more precisely the lack of wealth, works in reverse here.

Many children are living at the poverty level, where basic needs for food, water, shelter, and safety are in jeopardy, yet they yearn to be able to attend school and learn to read and write. They seem to understand that the path to survival, to a better existence, is through obtaining an education and the skills to be successful in our complex world.

One global voice from India explained that in India education is valued very much. "Parents make sacrifices for their children." In contrast, he explained that "in the U.S. there are too many distractions here, kids have too many freedoms, too much money and too much time. In India children must get back home and help out within the family" (personal communication).

Also, parents didn't pay kids for doing chores, as might occur in the United States and other Western cultures. The child's important job is to study and get the best education possible. It's very much tied in with the family beliefs, the culture, and the rules of society (personal communication).

Along the same lines, children should not be paid to get good grades; they must work for the right reasons, for the rewards of doing good work, for the excitement and intrinsic rewards of learning, taking responsibility for oneself, one's education, one's future. So, too, with issues of prosperity are the realities of what happens.

In the United States we have seen over the past many decades an increase in the divorce rate. Family ties become weakened as children accept jobs far away from their family of origin. The responsibility to the extended family is more fragile, where new friends and careers take on a greater meaning.

Many parents have less time to spend with their children; many must work two jobs or are emotionally unavailable to supervise the education of their children. It does take the involvement of parents, community, and professionals to support the educational excellence of our children. Undoubtedly the interrelationship of the economic issues and our societal changes have impacted our children's academic success.

MORE SPECIFIC MONETARY BARRIERS

In addition to the broader economic issues there also are more specific monetary barriers to educational excellence, including teacher salaries, cost of
teacher preparation, and continuing education programs, the struggles with
teacher unions, the cost of building safe schools and updating and maintaining healthy environments, and the cost of equalizing educational opportunities for all children.

Teacher Salaries

Teacher salaries have been and will continue to be an enormous stumbling
block. We have seen how society's value of teachers is very high in other
educationally thriving countries, including China, Finland, Japan, Canada,
India, and even Morocco and the Ukraine (Global Research, Summit, 2011,
Sahlberg, 2011).

In the United States this is more an idea than a reality. We often express
an alarming saying, "Those who can't . . . teach." In other words, those who
have not been as successful in school and cannot get accepted to the competitive colleges go into teaching! Naturally, this is not the case with most of our
dedicated teachers, but it does reflect a very serious culture value—or rather
lack of value—for education.

Indeed, this too can be seen as an issue of prosperity . . . those who can do
so go into more lucrative lines of work! Living in the United States is expensive, and given our cultural background, we expect the good life. Unfortunately, teachers often need to work two or more jobs just to make ends meet.
This leaves little time or energy to devote to our children.

Other issues often further complicate the situation. Many hold onto teaching positions because of the job security, but their hearts are not in teaching.
Currently, schools get stuck keeping teachers who have lost their enthusiasm
and others who clearly are incompetent and not dedicated to their profession
and, in some cases, even harmful to the learning process of children.

Such teachers need to be given a chance to change and improve their
approaches, but they should not be allowed to remain, negatively affecting
the education of children year after year and absorbing much of the money,
which could go to more capable, dedicated teachers.

Teacher Education

> *Most teachers are trying to do good work, but they find themselves underprep-*
> *ared, essentially trying to bandage a hemorrhaging artery* (Gunzelmann,
> 2009).

This brings us to the next barrier to excellence. In our country, becoming a good teacher can be a demanding and expensive process. Many motivated young education students fall into serious debt trying to complete their undergraduate education leading toward teacher certification. Continuing their education to become graduate-level educators is often overwhelming financially, yet it is well educated teachers that we need.

Once having completed their education and landing their first teaching job, many new teachers begin in inner-city schools. Once they become experienced and even more valuable teachers, the best teachers often migrate from inner-city and rural schools to higher-paying suburban localities, a trend that further increases the inequity in our schools. Many leave the field of education altogether to take better paying jobs in different fields just to make ends meet and pay down student loans.

This is not the case in other thriving countries. For example, our interviews with students and teachers from other countries indicate that outside the United States, teachers are generally among the most valued leaders in their own societies. The literature reveals that in Finland, for example, teachers are selected for a tuition-free graduate-level teacher education program, complete with a living stipend (Forum, 2008, p. 27). Other countries have undertaken similar interventions. Shouldn't the United States be doing the same?

Research repeatedly indicates that good teachers are education's most important factor. Linda Darling-Hammond (2008) concurs that the most significant influence on learning is the teacher, since teachers influence a student's learning either positively or negatively for years (p. 34). Without a doubt, the most important results have all boiled down to the importance of the teacher.

An analysis of the results from the 2011 International Summit on the Teaching Profession, convened by the U.S. Department of Education with host organizations, including OECD, EI (Education International), NEA (National Education Association), AFT (American Federation of Teachers), CCSSO (Council of Chief State Schools Officers), and Asia Society, identified and discussed themes of teacher recruitment and preparation, development, support and retention of teachers, teacher evaluation and compensation, and teacher engagement and reform.

Without exception, educationally successful countries place the importance of teachers at a very high level. Teachers are trusted and enjoy a high degree of autonomy in these flourishing countries. They are selected from among the top academic performers in their countries and invited to become teachers . . . the noblest of professions (U.S. Department of Education, 2011).

American society must demonstrate respect for teachers through salary increases, benefits, tuition reimbursement, researched-based teacher preparation programs, and mentoring, as well as graduate and continuing education programs. (Teacher education programs need major revisions to meet the needs of the twenty-first-century learner as well, but this will be addressed in the next chapter.)

Unions

Unions for teachers seem to present another troublesome economic barrier to education in the United States . . . but possibly this is a needless wall. Certainly we can see the need for educators to have allies on their side to help negotiate salaries, health benefits, retirement, and issues of job security, especially during these economically difficult years. Our country has been built upon such labor representation and does not need to present the roadblocks that we are so often seeing.

The highest-performing countries, including Finland, Canada, and Singapore (among many others) work as a team between the teachers' unions and policy makers, which has resulted in flourishing changes (Walker, 2011). As we learned earlier, the International Summit on the Teaching Profession (March 2011) brought together education ministers, national union leaders, education organization leaders, and accomplished teachers from high-performing countries in order to identify best practices, and it was clear that the unions were working cooperatively and successfully with those involved.

Presently, the political troubles occurring in Ohio, Indiana, and Wisconsin over teachers' unions will likely crop up in others states as well, given the economic situation and many states that find themselves at the door of bankruptcy. Unions are not necessarily the problem . . . although clearly the unions need to work cooperatively with our government and vice versa in order to solve the economic issues. One side blaming the other only clouds the issues and interferes with needed changes.

This collective bargaining process is deeply ingrained in the history and culture of the United States and in fact is required as part of the curriculum in U.S. history. Given that we teach this in our schools, we should be able to model this process for our students.

Lawyers in the Schools

Along these same lines, we see an increased use of lawyers in our schools. Do not get me wrong; our legal system and our lawyers have played a strong role in helping to begin to equalize educational opportunities for all students whatever the race, creed, gender, or special need. Another book could easily be written on such landmark cases as *Brown v. Board of Education* and our laws protecting the rights of our students.

However, what presents as another barrier to educational excellence is what I term the *"educational legalese syndrome,"* which depletes much of the needed funding our schools need. Schools spend inordinate sums of money trying to keep one or two students out of specialized schools when in fact the student may well benefit from a year or two of a well-run special program and then be able to be successfully integrated back into the public school and flourish, and at far less expense in the long run.

Serious work needs to be done in this area. One needs always to keep in mind what is best for each student, how we can support each student to succeed. A lot of money will be saved, and more students will thrive.

Equality of Educational Opportunity

Equal educational opportunities must be made available for all students, whatever the gender, race, religion, creed, or socioeconomic level. The United States Constitution is built upon these principles . . . yet in reality, partially because of economic issues, this is most definitely not the case.

When talking about our schools, educational reformer Jonathan Kozol said: "All our children are of equal value in the eyes of God," . . . but there is no equality when it comes to education (2003). Here we are now some twenty years after Kozol's "Savage Inequalities." At the time Dr. Thomas Cottle wondered if we would find a country that would embrace and educate all its children (1992). I am sorry to say that although we have made some progress we have regressed in other areas. Dr. Cottle's and Dr. Kozol's concern for equity of education are still problematic.

A groundbreaking account from the Forum for Education and Democracy (2008), *Democracy at Risk* elaborates further on the unevenness and inequity that characterizes American education. According to the Forum, the United States is one of the most inequitable nations (p. vi). It was the government funding cuts from the 1980s that exacerbated the decline. Although some progress was again made in the 1990s, we still have a long way to go (pp. iv–v).

According to *Democracy At Risk* (Forum, 2008), the United States has one of the most inequitably funded education systems of all industrialized nations. There is now an alarming phenomenon called the "school-to-prison pipeline," which reportedly is in large part due to the inequity within our society (pp. 21–22). We see the potential of thousands being lost to the productiveness of our country and a resulting drain on our economic well-being. Our schools can play a large part in rectifying these problems for future generations if our schools are well funded.

The more affluent communities definitely have access to better public schools; they have better buildings; more facilities for sports, art, and music; and better cafeterias, auditoriums, libraries, and classrooms. They have access to much more technology, with computers that have Internet access for every student in the classroom, additional computer labs, well-equipped libraries, and no shortage of current textbooks and supplies.

This is not the case in many of our rural and inner-city schools. At times, textbooks are not even issued to students for fear that they will ruin the books . . . and probably not read them anyway. Technology, experienced teachers, educational materials, and safe school climates are not the norm in our less wealthy systems.

The inequity of education also relates to other economic factors besides the school differences. A report by the National Clearinghouse for Education Statistics, titled "Status and Trends in Education of Racial and Ethnic Minorities," analyzed the education of all major ethnic and racial groups in the United States from prekindergarten through postsecondary level.

Several factors were identified that correlated with the achievement gap between black and white students, including living in poverty (KewalRamani, Gilbertson, Fox, & Provasnik, 2007). A report by the Educational Testing Service (2010) acknowledged sixteen previously identified issues that correlated with how well students achieve in school. Some were school related and could be improved by our school personnel, educators, and federal funding policies . . . all requiring a strong economic foundation. These include rigorous curriculum and teacher preparedness.

PENNY-WISE AND POUND-FOOLISH—EDUCATIONAL POLICIES AND ECONOMICS

Although we will look in depth at educational issues in chapter 8, it is important to address several concerns here since they are so intertwined with monetary issues.

The business practice of rewarding success with bonuses tends to backfire when applied as merit pay for teachers. A quote from Hillary Clinton clearly articulates this problem:

> Merit pay to individual teachers would discourage teachers from helping troubled students and would create a distorted competition among teachers. I don't think that's a very good way to inspire teachers. We want our best teachers to work with the kids who are the hardest to teach. If teachers are going to be told that the people who look better on a test are the ones who are going to get them rewarded in salary or compensation, why would anyone take on the kids who are harder to teach? (*New York Times*, April 6, 2000, p. 25)

This brings us to the issue of testing glitches. Testing concerns also fall under this main economic category of educational policies and practices. A quotation from Alfie Kohn articulates many of these concerns:

> Our students are tested to an extent that is unprecedented in American history and unparalleled anywhere in the world. Politicians and businesspeople, determined to get tough with students and teachers, have increased the pressure to raise standardized test scores. Unfortunately, the effort to do so typically comes at the expense of more meaningful forms of learning. (Kohn, 2000)

Related to these issues are the economics behind our assessment movement. We must all become more aware that in the United States, testing is a huge business, and money moves the business world. Psychologists and educators know that it is wrong to make decisions based on a single test score.

Decisions should be based on a balanced, complete understanding of each child. Numbers and scores can be misleading if we don't consider the whole picture, which means using both qualitative and quantitative approaches . . . and multiple-choice formats just don't cut it. Yes, they save time and money . . . but at the expense of deeper learning and measuring problem-solving ability.

Yet because of economic, time, and political and social pressures, psychologists and educators are forced to rely more and more heavily on quantitative methods, and many have been deceived into believing that numbers tell the whole story. This is a very dangerous practice!

Across the United States, we have an unrelenting movement toward accountability, with the increased use of standardized tests and high-stakes testing. Along with these pressures come the harmful side effects of teaching to the test, test anxiety, lowered self-esteem, misunderstandings of children, and missed opportunities for many.

Hardly any countries in the world use standardized testing with children before the age of sixteen. In the United States we use such tests with young children even though we know that doing so is contradictory to research findings. Furthermore, few countries use multiple-choice formats with children of any age (Kohn, 2000; see also Kohn, 2004).

There is strong evidence that the increased use of standardized tests undermines student achievement and increases the distrust that many have for teachers, students, and students' own judgments (Meier, 2002). Additionally, parents may believe that teachers will see their children as less capable based upon faulty test scores, and students may doubt their own abilities by putting too much faith in the results of standardized tests that often do not show accurate proficiency.

The misunderstanding of testing develops into toxic situations for all affected by test scores: students, teachers, parents, administrators, and those in the entire school system and community. We know without a doubt that there is no one test that can determine a student's ability or achievement. Nor is there an assessment tool that can measure a teacher's or a school system's effectiveness. To use evaluation in this manner is a flagrant misuse of tests . . . and a practice that sets up a serious barrier to excellence.

CLASS SIZE

The number of students in a class is another economics-related issue. Reducing class size costs money because of the need for increased space and more teachers. Smaller classes do matter, although the research can be confusing on this issue because of school systems' overreliance on general statistics that look at large groups of students and then making decisions for all students.

Whitehurst and Chingos state the following:

> Because the pool of credible studies is small and the individual studies differ in the setting, method, grades, and magnitude of class size variation that is studied, conclusions have to be tentative. But it appears that very large class-size reductions, on the order of magnitude of 7–10 fewer students per class, can have significant long-term effects on student achievement and other meaningful outcomes. These effects seem to be largest when introduced in the earliest grades and for students from less advantaged family backgrounds. (Whitehurst & Chingos, 2011)

Even the most capable of teachers will have difficulty managing large classes of children with unique learning needs. Small classes are particularly important in the early grades, for children with special needs, and for students from lower economic backgrounds.

Frequently, out-of-control classrooms require more money since at times it may be in the best interest of all for a student to attend a specialized school. If it wasn't for a money issue, these students would not be allowed to rob others of learning while they themselves would be receiving the needed interventions, later to be integrated back into the regular classroom.

Many states have set guidelines for class size, but unfortunately these rules have been overlooked in the current economic crisis. Here again we have decisions made on the academic success of our children that are penny-wise and pound-foolish.

Other issues that fall into this penny-wise and pound-foolish category involve:

- Teachers' aides, usually with little or no training, are hired in the schools to work with the most challenged students because they can be hired at lower pay.

- Busing schedules are based upon economics rather than how/when students will learn best. For example, many teenage students are getting too little sleep due to biological changes that do not fit well with busing schedules or optimal early morning classes. Requiring high-school students to start much earlier, when medical research clearly shows the need for added sleep during these years and the different sleep/wake cycle for teens, does not seem a wise choice. Adolescents will learn best with nine to ten hours of sleep and classes later in the morning (National Sleep Foundation, 2007).
- Food in many U.S. school cafeterias is usually surplus and not the healthiest of choices for our children, but it is inexpensive! Many of our children are obese according to recent findings, and such food policies are not helping, along with not having enough time to exercise, relax, and socialize with other children during the very short lunchtime.

If we compare our lunchtimes with those in academically flourishing Finland, we are woefully inadequate. Children in Finland are served organic foods, family style, where teachers and students are encouraged to relax and socialize at mealtime, which is a full hour. Exercising and fresh air also are seen as important. Children return refreshed and ready to learn.

HOME AND FAMILY

The economics of home and family situations also has an impact on educational excellence. With issues of affluence come the realities of what happens . . . family ties become weakened as children accept jobs far away from their family of origin. The responsibility to the extended family is more fragile, where new friends and careers take on a greater meaning. And there are fragmented families with less time and support needed for the educational excellence of our children.

According to one interviewed global individual, "People who have seen hard times need to support one another and stay together. [This] can be good in the long run" (personal communication). What he meant by this statement is that it is only fairly recently, due to the expense of wars, defense, natural disasters, and global economic problems, that in the United States we have experienced more difficult financial times. For the most part, many families have not needed to support one another in a manner conducive to educational excellence.

Interestingly enough, this same individual was quite perplexed by the business of American youth and the fact that most youth in the United States work at least part-time while attending school (high-school through college-age). In other thriving countries a young person's job is to be the best student possible . . . again, here in the United States this is an added distraction and in many cases a necessity.

Research indicates that the differences between racial groups (specifically blacks and whites) appear to be primarily due to socioeconomic differences. It appears that white students' parents tend to have higher levels of education overall and earn more money . . . suggesting the perpetuation of problems from one generation to the next when inequities exist, according to Adam Gamoran and Daniel Long (2006) from the Wisconsin Center for Education Research (a part of the School of Education at the University of Wisconsin at Madison).

Furthermore, the soaring cost of a college/university education can be daunting for most parents and students alike in the United States. In many ways it may prevent some very capable young people from even trying. Again . . . this does not need to be the case, as we have seen in many other countries. Other higher-performing nations provide the out-of-school learning supports, including child care, free, nutritious lunches, safe buildings, superior teachers, educational supportive interventions, and health and dental care (Forum, 2008, p. vi).

Clearly our high rate of unemployment and the current economic crisis are not going to help equalize the playing field without appropriate interventions. Without a doubt it will take a generation of better schools, attainment of higher education, and equal status and pay in jobs to turn this situation around . . . but it can begin now, and it is manageable.

HEALTHY AND SAFETY ISSUES

Keeping our schools safe and healthy requires money . . . there's no way around this issue. If we want our students to thrive, this is essential to their well-being.

Many of our nation's school facilities are outdated, with problems such as asbestos, lead paint, air quality problems, and a host of environmental contaminants. Even in our newer buildings, there are real causes for concern. Some new schools have been built on landfills with toxic chemicals right below the surface . . . all because the price was right.

Furthermore, our country is growing rapidly. According to information from the U.S. Census Bureau (2010), the U.S. population reached 281,421,906 in 2000 with current estimates over 299,000,000 (Population Reference Bureau, 1999). Furthermore, the Census Bureau (2010) claims that the population is rising rapidly and will continue to do so. With statistics such as these, we undoubtedly have a growth problem and a real predicament with providing safe and first-rate schools for our nation's children.

All could be corrected with the necessary monetary resources. Other countries have done so, and so can we! One of the best examples comes from educationally soaring Finland, where schools are environmentally friendly, bright, and comfortable. We can and must provide the same for our children. The cost of a wasted education is much too high.

Chapter Seven

Psychological Barriers to Educational Excellence

Freedom is . . . the ability to think on your own and to pursue your own path as far as your gifts can take you— and only education can give you that freedom, can open those doors.
—U.S. Secretary of Education Arne Duncan

This is a lovely statement of the ideal of education in our country. Without a doubt our freedom is intricately involved with our pursuit of education. However, there are numerous psychological barriers that interfere with our ability to pursue our own paths. Since psychology can be defined as the study of human thoughts, emotions, and behavior, it is important to analyze our way of thinking, feeling, and being in the United States in terms of both the broader concepts and the individual, including parents, teachers, administrators, and the students.

Each and every one of us sets up our own unique barriers to educational excellence as a result of our psyche and the broader psychological issues of our colleagues involved in education. It will take each one of us to make our own personal changes, to understand ourselves and others better in order to break down the barriers that stand in the way of excellence.

WIDESPREAD PSYCHOLOGICAL ISSUES

Our thoughts, emotions, and behaviors guide our educational policies and practices. These customary issues impact parents, teachers, administrators, politicians, and the community, and thus they impact our schools. The psychological barriers can be further broken down into the subcategories of cognitive, emotional, and behavioral areas, allowing for finer analysis. (I identify several to illustrate the barriers. You may identify more from your own reflections.)

For example, *cognitive walls* involve our thought processes, some of which we may be aware, while others may be in our subconscious or unconscious realm. Are we in denial of how serious the educational problems are in the United States? Do we believe that we still lead the world academically? Do we believe that others should learn our language and that we do not need to understand our global neighbors? These are a few of the cognitive barriers in need of modification.

The discussion of such cognitive barriers may not ring true when we first hear them, particularly if they are not in our conscious thoughts . . . yet by reading, researching, and analyzing, we are planting the seeds for growth, for awareness of how our thought processes can hinder our success.

The *emotional barriers* involve our feelings about situations and issues involved in failing, or shall we say falling far short of educational excellence. Emotions may involve fear or anger, resentment . . . all disguising the issues at hand . . . all a defensive barrier preventing us from seeing the importance of our educational problems.

The *behavior blockages* involve our actions, what we do. Shall we continue to do the same old things that have not worked, or is it time to begin new research-based approaches? Doing nothing is also a behavioral barrier preventing excellence.

Deep-Seated Cognitive Barriers

1. Thoughts about research, statistics, and testing are first on the list of cognitive barriers. Many professionals are stuck on the idea that statistics tell the whole story. Well, they don't! Statistics are very important in research and can show us trends and relationships, and with experimental research can even indicate cause.

However, using only quantitative research methodology can be misleading. Statistics don't tell us about why individual students are not learning, or why some teachers and schools are more successful than others. To get at the complexity of these questions requires qualitative methods that can begin to grasp the very essence of the educational experience.

Such qualitative studies then must be further researched, and here's where statistics are essential to indicate whether indeed there is a relationship and to show what factors are actually needed for learning excellence. In other words, a balance of research is required . . . one without the other is inadequate.

Additionally, we must have a balanced approach from research from many fields relating to the health and development of children, learning, school climate, teacher education, curriculum and educational approaches, and the broader issues of our society, economy, and country. (Interestingly enough, few teachers are trained in conducting research in the United States!)

Then we have instances of misunderstanding of research and/or the misapplication of research. A case in point deals with the self-esteem movement that developed in the late 1960s with a research project done by Stanley Coopersmith (1967), a project that was misunderstood and misapplied in the field of education. Coopersmith, a psychologist, believed that raising children's self-esteem was important in proper child rearing, but his results correlated well with sage, old child-rearing practices that require clear rules and enforced limits in order for children to develop high self-esteem.

Unfortunately, many educators took this to mean that children should always be praised even when they were only doing mediocre work. The children figured out very quickly that they did not need to work as hard . . . and the false praise actually eroded their self-esteem!

We also can see this unreasonable reliance on numbers with the testing crisis we currently find ourselves in. We have learned previously that test scores can be misleading and that at times in the United States these scores have been used in ways that the tests were not designed to measure. Bottom line: the results are invalid and unreliable when used in this manner. The psychological issue at hand is how we think about numbers and testing.

There is too much emphasis placed on tests and competing in the world academic arena as well. The focus really needs to be more on working together, finding out what each individual is about, and assisting with maximizing learning overall. Working together . . . not working against one another is key. These comments concur with the work of Wagner (2008) as well as many others.

2. Reflections upon our own early educational experiences. Next we should look at what happens when we think back upon our own education. We may believe such declarations as, "Well, it was good enough for me," or "That's the way it has always been done." Such cognitions are barriers to excellence, and they keep us stuck doing the same old things that just are no longer working!

Reluctance to change is really part of our human nature. We become comfortable with familiar routines, and we believe that we must be doing all right because that's the way schools have always operated. It is difficult to acknowledge that our beliefs, our policies, and the approaches that we've been educated and trained to use might not always be best.

Undoubtedly, most of us in the fields of education and psychology want to help the children with whom we work. This resistance can be overcome if we acknowledge that there is a problem, stop blaming, and change what we can.

3. Students are not to be trusted, or so some believe. This brings us to the third broad cognitive barrier. Many educators believe that students cannot be trusted to do the right thing, to want to learn and to take responsibility for their learning. We may not want to believe this is true, but all we need do is look at our school policies on discipline, attendance, and expectations.

Our expectations are set at a minimum of what students should do—how many pages they should read, how much time they should spend on their homework, how many days they can miss from school. So what do students do? They do what is expected . . . the minimum. If we can change our thought process to believe that most students want to learn and most students are responsible, and raise our expectations . . . we may see a largely different outcome.

4. I think most readers will agree that the majority of teachers and administrators really want to do good work. They want our students to learn, to excel, and they want to feel a sense of satisfaction from the work. Yet many teachers may not think about how important they are to our children.

They may think they are insignificant because they are paid less than those in many other professions. This inaccurate and damaging thought process could lead to teachers becoming indifferent, less motivated, and thinking about their career as educator as just a job to make ends meet, rather than as one of the most important jobs in our country!

Widespread Emotional Barriers

1. Without a doubt, one of the themes that appears to underlie our psychological barriers is that of fear. Anxiety seems to be an emotion that penetrates all levels of our psychological nature . . . sometimes without our even being aware. Fear is a pervasive emotion that is primal in nature and thus can override our intellect. Fear, when rational, is meant to protect us, to ensure survival. Yet fear can have counterproductive side effects.

Why are we so afraid as a people? Our motto is the home of the strong and the home of the brave. This is true . . . but underneath lies a rather free-floating anxiety. In today's world there are many more threats than there used to be and more reasons to be on our guard.

I am startled when I listen to college freshmen and U.S. high-school students talk about their fears of what will happen when they get to college if they don't do this or they don't do such-and-such. These students have had the added stress of their parents and teachers worrying that if the students do not perform well academically, they will not get into the best colleges, that the school will be labeled as not having met adequate yearly progress, and so on.

Most are just idle threats, but they can and do turn kids off to learning. If these threats become a part of the student's belief system, they may actually impede learning by increasing anxiety too much or having kids give up in frustration.

Fear also blocks creativity. Most children are naturally curious, but the longer they attend formal schooling it seems that their creativity decreases. Yet it is creativity and innovative thinkers that we need for the twenty-first century. Students need to be able to think outside the box, to solve problems, to rely on their own intellect, and to be able to work cooperatively together. Tony Wagner (2008), author of *The Global Achievement Gap*, appears to agree with these findings. (We will hear more about this in chapter 9.)

Without a doubt, too much stress can and does interfere with optimal performance. Some stress is necessary, but too much negatively impacts students' learning. So why do we instill fear in our students? Is it some sort of tainted attempt to motivate? Without a doubt, fear shuts down learning and is a major barrier to excellence. Threats and punishment backfire. Students may spend a minimum of time looking at a book . . . but the anxiety, anger, and resentment that build up short-circuit real and deep learning.

2. The second emotional barrier involves cynicism. Distrust seems to be woven into the very fabric of our schools in the United States. Frequently, schools and teachers face legal difficulties, schools and teachers get improperly evaluated, and it appears we don't seem to trust our students either. We do not believe they can take responsibility for their learning or know when they need to take care of their basic needs of eating or toileting. Hall passes are needed to go to the restrooms, the library, or the school nurse.

There is also a distrust . . . almost a sense of unfounded arrogance that our way is the best way. We really do need to start listening to the successes of other countries with their educational approaches.

We have taken away the students' responsibility for thinking as well. They are told what they must learn, what the right answers are to the test questions, and that the end grade (score) is what is most important.

3. There also is a degree of denial occurring in our schools. Denial is a defensive mechanism, usually operating at an unconscious level, in protection of our egos. Such defense strategies are not really problematic unless they are a primary mode of thinking. Are some of us in the schools denying that there are serious problems? I wonder.

In the case of our schools and all those involved, denial may be operating to protect from the increasing fear and stress. For example, are students in denial of what is at stake if they do not take responsibility for their learning, if they believe that there is plenty of time for learning when they are older?

Are our politicians in denial of the central importance of education to our country, that it is not wise to cut needed funds to our schools? Are our teachers and administrators in denial that our approaches are outdated and that our teacher preparation programs are not adequate? Are some parents in denial that their career is more important than time spent with their child? Do they not understand that love, support, and time spent with children is their most essential job? Clearly this needs to stop!

Broad Behavioral Barriers

The cognitive and emotional barriers discussed thus far result in problematic behaviors, including avoidance of the issues, throwing in the towel on trying to make the needed changes, not putting education at the top of the list on the country's priorities, and blaming others for the problems (students for not learning, parents for lack of involvement or overinvolvement, or society for a whole cluster of related issues). Such defensive behavior is not conducive to solving our country's education problems. Instead, it sets up another barrier to excellence.

PSYCHOLOGY OF THE STUDENT

Students deserve a section all on their own because we can research, theorize, implement changes, assess, and revise all we want. Without understanding the students, all is futile.

Cognitive Student Barriers

I do wonder why so many of our students develop a strong dislike, even a hatred, for school. When entering kindergarten and first grade, most students are excited and love school. Slowly over the next few years, their thoughts most definitely seem to change, erecting a barrier to learning that is difficult for teachers to break through.

Another strange belief seems to be that so many students believe it is the teacher's responsibility to make them learn. Of course it is the teacher's job to teach and to teach well . . . but a wall is built that often is insurmountable when students are not held responsible for their learning.

Along these same lines is a common student belief that there is always time to get serious about learning later. Little are they aware how learning is a cumulative process and requires consistency . . . not something that is a semester cram job.

Naturally, some of these cognitions may result from students believing that they are less capable than others or possibly even the belief that in some manner they are more advanced than others, resting a bit on the laurels of their parents' and grandparents' accomplishments and the reputation of the United States as a world leader . . . a title no longer held in the field of education.

Emotional Student Barriers

Students' cognitions are closely linked to their feelings and thus influence their behaviors. Unfortunately, we are seeing more children in our schools with anxiety disorders, depression, lowered self-esteem, behavioral disorders, learning difficulties, and a fear of failure/fear of success phenomenon that further interferes with excellence in learning (Gunzelmann, 1983; Unpublished doctoral dissertation).

Possibly our students are not feeling emotionally safe in our schools, at home, or with themselves. It seems safe to say that it appears that some of their emotional issues are created from self-defeating thoughts and behaviors.

Behavioral Student Barriers

Students' cognitions coupled with their emotions lead to many self-defeating behaviors, including defensive behavior, acting cool, pretending that school is not important, and turning off to education or dropping out altogether.

Another behavioral obstacle that complicates school in the United States and is frequently talked about in the news is the concept of adolescent "storm and stress." Some believe it is natural for teenagers to go through periods of stress, rebelliousness, and being argumentative . . . that it is a necessary rite of passage. Yet in many other cultures this is not the case (Arriaga & Rangwala, 2006).

Clearly there are other psychological issues that interfere with our educational excellence in the United States. My point with this chapter was to stimulate the reader with several concrete examples of psychological issues that start students on a downward spiral of faulty thinking, emotional conflict, and self-defeating behavior, creating blockages to learning.

Chapter Eight

Educational Issues

Process and Logistical Barriers

The manner in which we plan, procure, maintain, and transport our educational material and personnel makes up the logistical barriers, while the process-related barriers involve more approach and procedural barriers to educational excellence. As we proceed through chapter 8 we will become more aware of the quagmire of problems our schools face and how each barrier is quite muddled with the other barriers discussed so far. Indeed, it is why it has been so difficult to find a solution to our educational woes.

PROCESS-RELATED BARRIERS

The best place to begin to explain the barriers that occur in this category is to start well before teachers even enter a classroom. Teachers are the number one most important factor related to academic success (Forum, 2011). And it is at this beginning phase that we see our U.S. system encountering problems.

Most teachers have memories from their own years as students. In some cases this is a benefit, but for the most part the memories have been of outdated models, which further contributes to our obsolete system. Not only do our students need an education for the twenty-first century, so do our teachers!

Teacher Preparation

Teacher preparation programs need to be revamped here in the United States. Sometimes students want to be teachers because of a sincere desire to help others learn. Oftentimes students may go into teaching for the wrong reasons. Although it certainly is not for the money, I have heard reasons such as the courses being easier, teachers getting good benefits, and so on.

Students wanting to become teachers really need to be extremely capable academically and highly motivated to become teachers for excellence. Acceptance into college or university teacher preparation programs really should be highly competitive and based upon a multifaceted admissions process.

Once in college, the academic focus needs to be on research methods, both qualitative and quantitative approaches, and on students'experience in conducting their own research as well. Psychology coursework in learning, educational psychology, child and adolescent development and assessment, and testing are essential . . . and, believe it or not, are almost always not required!

Curriculum in Our Schools

Sometimes the barriers to excellence involve the actual content of the curriculum, and at other times the barriers seem to involve the manner in which curriculum is implemented. Take, for example, the manner in which curriculum is established. It seems in other academically thriving countries the educational curriculum is set by the ministry of education (or other comparable government organizations).

In the United Sates this process works a bit differently. We have read about our government-set policies such as No Child Left Behind and Race to the Top in previous chapters. Then we have the U.S. Department of Education, and each state has its own department of education. Each state must have accountability plans, curriculum standards, and so forth.

Naturally there are pros and cons to each approach. However, standards do need to be determined, and schools need to be able to assure learning without letting the hurdles the U.S. educational system currently must struggle with detract from learning success. Teachers need to be top notch, better prepared, well respected, and determined to make a positive difference in the lives of the children in their care. Politicians, policy makers, administrators, and parents need to do their parts to clear the barriers so that teachers can do their work successfully.

Once curriculum is determined, there are still many other barriers. For example, let's take a closer look at how foreign languages are taught here in the United States. Having spoken with guidance counselors and teachers about this issue, it seems we do not usually teach a foreign language to our students with the goal developing fluency with the language. It is more about learning a bit about the culture.

In one case, an outcome might be to be able to identify the Eiffel Tower! Clearly this is not developing an in-depth understanding of the culture at all. As far as the language competency is concerned, most U.S. students are fortunate if they can speak a few phrases in any second language.

This does not happen in other cultures, where students are expected to learn different languages (often more than one or two). Many students are able to communicate in the languages when they graduate. I have not interviewed students or teachers from any other country where foreign language fluency was not a primary focus.

We also see differences regarding when foreign languages are started in the schools. We may want to review the work of Lev Vygotsky and the windows of opportunity. Basically, if we want children to learn to speak a different language fluently, then studies should begin quite early. Waiting until middle school is counterproductive. Such decisions often are based upon economic issues of paying the salary of foreign language teachers for early ages.

Then we have the issue of continuity with curriculum here in the United States. So often students will take one class in geography and that is all, while in other countries they may take geography every year, each year building more and more depth to their knowledge and understanding. The U.S. approach of one course in a subject does not provide for reinforcement of material over time, which is necessary for permanent learning to occur.

Quite often, I hear students say that they are glad that they never need to take another math class again, believing that one year or even just one semester of geometry is more than enough. This type of curriculum planning sets up problems for students. First of all, there is much less depth. Second, students do not see the connections with other areas of study nor the importance of learning each subject to the best of their ability. After all, they can put geometry or geometry behind them and not think about that subject again!

Another problem involves the downward spiraling of the curriculum, expecting younger and younger students to learn abstract terms and concepts that they are not yet capable of grasping. Keeping the developmental perspective in mind is essential with curriculum planning, and scores of years of research backs the necessity of a developmental approach.

Academic policies such as trying to encourage the joy of reading also can create well-intentioned but detrimental roadblocks. Take, for example, a teaching policy of assigning a specific number of pages to read from a chosen book for enjoyment and then giving the assignment of stopping every few pages to write content answers to who, what, when, where, and why questions. This certainly is a damaging approach to encouraging reading for pleasure.

One teacher's explanation for this was to not overwhelm the struggling students, but unfortunately, it lowers the expectations for all students, as the tendency is to do the minimum or the assigned amount.

It became very clear from the interviews conducted during my global research that elements that we often believe to be so crucial to academic achievement just do not have as much impact as we once believed. It seems one of the most important elements is to have high expectations for our learners.

Achievement motivation research in the psychology field has identified the necessary ingredients for children to have a high achievement motivation (Schultz & Schultz, 2008). Certainly there can be an ultimate goal to strive toward, but then this must be broken down into meaningful steps, each with a subgoal that is a stretch for students, but not an impossible reach. Step by step, students can and will reach the higher goals with an intrinsic need to achieve deeper and deeper learning without suppressing the child's natural curiosity.

Testing has been discussed in depth in other chapters, but it needs another mention here as well. It seems preposterous, but teachers are not trained in assessment and testing practices, with the exception of some very simple briefing in classroom assessment techniques. Very few classroom teachers in the United States can explain the differences between types of assessment, standard deviations, and other simple statistical data, or even concepts such as reliability and validity. This lapse needs to be remediated.

Testing can be a barrier if misused, as we have seen in previous chapters. However, testing, when well constructed and used appropriately, can give us invaluable information regarding how we should teach each child, what information needs additional reinforcement, and so on.

Labeling and Diagnosis

Other interesting differences between education in the United States and education in many other thriving countries involve differences in perspective regarding students with special needs. Here in the United States there is a tendency to overlabel. We learned in *Hidden Dangers to Kids' Learning* that in some schools there is an superfluity of children with a label, and these students often tend to become their diagnosis along with all the helplessness and other negative side effects that may result from believing they are less capable or defective.

Certainly, obtaining a diagnosis is helpful in most instances . . . when there is a remedy for the disorder. But more often than not in the learning of children, that is not the case, and labels are harmful and often wrong. The label becomes the reason without other possible contributing factors being considered and changed.

Unfortunately, this is not an unusual development. Children who seem deficient or different because they learn differently, who are not learning up to expectations, or who are not behaving as anticipated are frequently misunderstood. "This mislabeling, misperception or blaming of the child is not done intentionally, but it frequently happens as a matter of routine, without looking at other possible causes, because the child may exhibit some characteristic symptoms of a disorder. Nevertheless, the misunderstanding and overuse of diagnosis can be at tremendous cost to the child" (Gunzelmann, 2011b). (See *Hidden Dangers to Kids' Learning* for a more in-depth analysis of the dangers of labeling.)

In other educationally successful countries we do see a difference in approach to children with special needs. In Finland, for example, teachers do not look for what is wrong with the child but more toward what they need to do to help the child learn. A label is not necessary. Special education is available for every child through personalized support. (Sahlberg, 2011).

Other countries (which shall remain nameless here) have been known to go to the other extreme by not understanding individual differences and using approaches such as shame or punishment, which can create a barrier to learning at the other extreme (personal communication). Naturally, this would not be tolerated in our culture.

Discipline and Behavior Management Issues

Another problematic area in the U.S. schools involves the degree of focus on discipline. It seems the expectation in our schools is that students should not be trusted and that they will misbehave if not controlled by rigid rules. Many students need to be given more responsibility and can be depended upon to behave.

Unfortunately, these capable students are infantilized and develop a sense of dependency that is not healthy. We see this phenomenon frequently in the schools . . . particularly when students get to secondary levels. They question constantly, "How long should this paper be?" "Will this be on the test?" It seems as if they literally cannot think for themselves.

On the other hand, there are many students who will obligingly and willingly rise to our distrustful expectations and misbehave. Either way, not trusting our students sets in motion a barrier to learning and is a high cost to pay for a quiet classroom.

Such management approaches actually breed anger and resentment and literally take the responsibility for learning and self-discipline away from the child. Time for teaching is taken up with trying to control the students . . . learning becomes secondary. Also, behaviorally disordered students may be negatively reinforced for their out-of-control behavior by teachers spending so much time with them.

Technology

Technology is here to stay. Many look at it as a distraction to education. Yet I do not see technology as a barrier to excellence; in many ways it is a way toward excellence if used well. Technology itself is neutral: the barrier is not knowing how to integrate it well into our educational programs or not having equal access to technology.

On the other hand, most American students are quite sophisticated with the use of many technologies and indeed may not always use them for attaining academic excellence. However, it is the way so many students learn and can be used quite effectively for all students in the classrooms. According to Dr. Chris Dede from Harvard University, emerging technologies are reshaping shifts in knowledge and skills that society values, developing new methods of teaching and learning as well as changing the characteristics of learners (Dede, 2011).

Additionally, technology allows for access to the best teachers on a subject, helping to equalize education in the United States as well as providing the most current information. We no longer need to be limited by a specific location, time, subject, or perspective. Technology can help us break down all barriers! Teachers need to guide students to ascertain which information is the most accurate, the best research, and so on. Technology will not put teachers out of work but will require our teachers to be much more highly trained.

Exercise, Relaxation, and Healthy Food

Exercise and relaxation are also essential to optimal learning. Regular exercise is not only a boon to maintaining healthy weight and strength; it is very helpful to attention span and learning. Children require regular activity, several times a day; exercise increases learning and focus while decreasing frustration and even the growing obesity problem with our children.

Nonetheless, what do our schools do? Recess is cut from the schedule as children reach middle school, and also the requirement for physical education may be as little as two semesters throughout all four years of high school. Yet cutting-edge research clearly shows the positive correlation between exercise and learning (Ratey, 2008).

Even basic policies on eating need revision. Children need nutritious and balanced food, and they need it more frequently than adults. Many children require several small, healthy meals throughout the day. However, the school schedule does not allow for this need.

The same holds true for lunchtime, a break in the day to refuel one's body with healthy foods, relax, and socialize a bit with friends. But this is not what happens here in U.S. schools. Lunchtime is very rushed, with students having about twenty-plus minutes to stand in line, get their food, and swallow some of it down . . . much is wasted. Many schools enforce quiet lunch periods as a form of discipline or punishment. This is not the relaxing, stress-reducing time that students require.

Nor are there many healthy food choices for students. School lunches are notorious for high-calorie fat and sugar content, further contributing to the problems of obesity and lack of nutritious, replenishing food.

Yet again, this is not the case in many academically thriving countries. Of course, in Finland we see the ideal: organic food served family style, and a leisurely hour's lunch to relax and socialize with friends and teachers (Finnish National Board of Education, 2008). But even in countries such as India, where money is less available, children bring their lunches from home. They do not consume fast foods to which so many of our children are addicted.

A good school canteen encourages pupils to enjoy an unhurried meal and offers them healthy choices. A pleasant, quiet dining area allows pupils to take their time and helps them to understand the role of eating, meal times and spending time with each other in promoting their well-being.

LOGISTICAL BARRIERS

In this section we will deal with barriers that are related to planning, maintaining, and facilitating the running of our schools, although it should be clear that it is difficult to always separate logistics from procedures.

Scheduling and Time-Related Issues

Issues of time most definitely come under the logistical barriers. Because time is limited, it too is a barrier to educational excellence if we are not able to modify and adjust our schedules. We briefly heard of the time issue related to eating, recess, and lunches . . . but there are many other areas as well.

The scheduling of subjects, one right after the other, is another pitfall. While this practice may be practical in some regards, it makes no sense at all from a deeper learning approach. Many students need time to think and reflect upon what they have just been taught, while others may still be deep in the process of trying to grasp a concept. Unfortunately, the bell rings, and learning stops. (In reality, learning stops well before the buzzer sounds since students are anticipating the bell.)

For example, consider the time issue involved with the problem of busing students to the schools. It need not be so problematic, but as usual, the bottom line on busing comes down to an economic issue rather than what is best for the students. (Again our priorities are out of whack.) Clearly, economic barriers play a role here. However, the students should not need to pay the price of decreased learning due to a busing schedule.

Adolescent research clearly indicates the need for at least eight hours of sleep for adolescents. The issue is not one of saying that these students should just get to sleep earlier. Biologically their clocks are set to stay awake longer at night and sleep later in the mornings. Their most effective time for school to start would be more toward 10:00 a.m. (National Sleep Foundation, 2007).

Most U.S. high schools start early, usually around 7:30 a.m. or earlier, which means that many adolescents are getting up by 5:30 or 6:00 a.m. to finish homework and get on the school bus. Without the required hours of sleep per night, they run an increased risk of depression and having attention issues, along with a decrease in learning, not to mention a higher risk of car accidents for those sleepy students who have their driver's license.

On the other hand, younger children are up and alert much earlier . . . these are the children that should be learning earlier and then out of school earlier in the afternoon. Yes, it would be an inconvenience for parents to be up and out with their children at the bus stops, but if learning is our goal, we need to pay attention to the varying times in development in which children learn optimally.

The response from our school committees is to begin the academic day earlier and earlier—based not on research, which clearly states what is best for the child, but on a budget and time issue, thus creating a barrier to success.

There are other time barriers as well. The length of the school day, school week, and school year are all involved here. Interestingly enough, in Finland, one of the world leaders in educational excellence, the students have one of the shortest school days of any country (Hancock, 2011). The time is well spent in school. The lack of time for reflection is another time-related barrier. If we really want students to learn at deeper levels, not merely memorize information to pass a multiple-choice test, then we need to build in time for reflection. It must become a part of the process for learning for synthesizing our understanding and then being able to take our understanding to the next creative step of problem solving.

It seems in the U.S. schools there is a fear that we are wasting time if every minute is not accounted for in full. The concern seems related to taking time away from learning more facts . . . from doing better on standardized tests, when in reality, this overscheduling is not allowing for time to deepen the learning.

Insightful levels of learning require a more relaxed schedule in order for students to be able to integrate learning and to allow for creative ideas to develop. Although some people think better under pressure, reflective thinking requires time and cannot be commanded on schedule.

Age Barriers

Age barriers are closely related to time barriers. Similar to the other areas discussed, we need to know what questions to ask in order to identify such barriers. For example:

- Does schooling need to be only a certain number of years?
- Why can't students learn material when they are ready and at their own pace?
- Why should students be denied education based upon age (either too young . . . or too old)?
- How have these arbitrary ages been established regarding readiness to start school?

It's interesting to note that in Finland children do not start school before age seven (Hancock, 2011). Requiring more years in school, longer days, and lengthier school years is not really necessary to attain excellence. It would probably add to the stress level of both teachers and students and may potentially have a negative impact.

Safe and Healthy Buildings

Even the physical layout of the school building and classrooms needs to be considered. The products used in building and in renovations and upkeep are problematic in many of our nation's schools. For example, we are seeing an increase in asthma in children at a time when many schools are being identified as having dangerous levels of molds and other pollutants. Such physical conditions interfere with the ability to learn and may be compounded by days missed from school and side effects from medication . . . not to mention lifelong implications.

When new schools are being constructed, careful planning must go into the specifications and thus include information from architects and builders, along with research from the fields of education, psychology, and medicine to address these concerns. Successful schools require the knowledge and support from a variety of experts.

By now the reader must think that this truly is an insurmountable tangled web . . . but there are answers. Some will be more long term, but many can be started today . . . by each and every one of us. Each and every one of us can make a difference . . . for that is how real change occurs. After all, we are the home of the brave, and we do not back down in the face of a challenge. So let's get started on the solutions.

Part III

Toward Educational Excellence and Beyond

Chapter Nine

Breaking Down the Barriers and Restoring Balance

Without a doubt, there are a myriad factors relating to our culture, our political system, our economic problems, psychological attributes, and educational policy, procedures, and logistical issues that could be tweaked to help cope with these issues. Certainly we have challenges to face to overcome these barriers and to restore balance to our schools . . . but Americans work best when challenged.

STEP I: AWARENESS—FOSTERING OF ESSENTIAL QUALITIES

We have already taken the first step by becoming aware that there is indeed a serious educational situation in the United States. We have identified numerous barriers that interplay with one another in a negative synergistic manner. We need to make others aware of the seriousness of the problems faced by our schools.

STEP II: OVERCOMING RESISTANCE

Educating our children for academic excellence is our most important challenge. To do this, we must make changes. However, resistance to change is natural; it is a part of human nature. There are many who may think that the way we have always educated our children, the way they were educated, was good enough for them and thus it should be good enough today. Yet there is

no way we can deny the facts: the United States is not keeping up educationally; our children are not prepared for college or for careers in our twenty-
first-century world.

Step II, therefore, involves fostering the following qualities in all those
involved with the education of our children, for it is these qualities that will
allow for needed changes.

Qualities Essential to Overcome Resistance and Make Needed Changes

Our inductive reasoning abilities need to be revitalized in order to understand
that we have a problem, to ask the right questions, and to satisfy an insatiable
need (curiosity) to find the answers. Real curiosity often leads to pleasure in
learning and a renewed sense of pleasure and awe in our work as well. It is
essential to foster and maintain this quality for the adults, as well as for the
children.

1. *Open-mindedness*: We need to make changes to our educational system. The ways we have been educating our youth are no longer working in the twenty-first century. We need to maintain an open mind to
   the research from interdisciplinary fields and to the possibility that
   educators in other countries may have knowledge that is helpful to us
   as well.
2. *Curiosity*: The need to question and the need to find answers has been
   one of the hallmarks of our society. Yet in recent generations with
   movements toward "teaching to the test" and the downing of the curriculum, the curiosity factor has been suppressed.
3. *Analytical Abilities*: Along the same lines, our analytical abilities need
   to be fine-tuned so that we are better able to analyze the data and to
   synthesize the research into meaningful, helpful information. We need
   to keep abreast of the current research in our fields, consult with
   professionals outside our fields, and acknowledge our limitations.
4. *Work Ethic*: Our solid work ethic needs to be reinstated. We may
   possess all the intellectual ability and inquisitiveness, but without the
   determination, focus, and needed support to work hard . . . little will
   be gained. Practice is paramount if we are to bridge the gap we currently have between research and application in the field.
5. *Flexibility*: Realize that failure, disappointment, and setbacks are a
   part of the growing and learning process. There is no one right answer
   for all children; there is no one best approach. There are certain elements we know are essential for all children, but we must maintain
   flexibility to cope with individual difference toward the goal of com-

petency, without punishment, fear of poor grades, or low test scores. When schools, teachers, and students are struggling, they need to be supported, not reprimanded.

6. *Respect and Appreciation of Diversity*: A firm belief is essential that it is through difference that we grow, that we can help each child become who he or she was meant to be, to contribute to our society in his or her unique and positive manner—not to become an automated machine. It is our differences, our unique views of the world and approaches to problem solving that will contribute to our twenty-first-century society.

With these qualities in hand we can begin to break down these barriers and rebalance our system, restoring educational excellence for our children and the future of our country.

STEP III: BREAKING DOWN THE BARRIERS AND REGAINING BALANCE

As former president Ronald Reagan said on June 12, 1987, at the Brandenburg wall . . . "Tear down this wall!" so too we must break down the invisible walls preventing excellence in the U.S. educational system. When we break down any barrier, we must have a plan to rebuild and understand that there may be some ups and downs during a transitional time, during the rebalancing period. (These down periods, or growing pains, should not be seen as setbacks but as a part of our rebalancing to achieve excellence.)

An analysis of each of the barriers with research-based answers is in order at this point.

We can see by the diagram that each of the barriers is related to all the others. When the barriers are removed and the system rebalanced, there can exist a flow from one area to another, working together collaboratively toward a gold star of educational excellence. (Note the star shape that forms when all areas are working cooperatively together!)

Societal and Cultural Barriers

Our societal and cultural barriers are quite complex, as we have seen, and there is interaction between each barrier. Most barriers are needless: indeed, we may realize that they are not really barriers at all until they get out of balance and prohibit excellence.

As we saw in chapter 4, the work ethic was central to our society in our early history. As we became more prosperous (clearly an economic issue), many of our people began to enjoy leisure time. As generations have passed,

Figure 9.1 Analysis & Solutions Barrier By Barrier

each a bit more affluent than the one before, we have lost sight of the importance of hard work to learn, be successful, and feel a real sense of esteem.

Regaining the balance to this important value requires breaking down the idea that success equals leisure and entitlement, rather than excellence is obtained through hard work. Holding each individual responsible for his or her education and helping each to see the value and importance of education, the great gift that they can earn will take time.

Giving back to one's community through volunteer and community service is one manner to start to dismantle this barrier. It also will require a mind-set shift, understanding that a teacher's job is not to force-feed unmotivated students to learn. It is the student's responsibility to engage, and the teacher's responsibility to teach, guide, and monitor the process.

Rebalancing is also in order when we go too far in one direction. Diagnosing each little difference in the medical field can be most helpful under certain circumstances. However, it is not necessary in an educational setting if each child is understood for his or her strengths and weaknesses and assisted to learn in a manner appropriate to his or her needs. This can be done without a label. We all have differences in our abilities and our approaches to learning and as such should be taught in ways that maximize our learning.

The value of education also has changed within the United States, as we saw in chapter 4. It's time to rebuild the culture of respect for our teachers. When we put our money where our mouths are, we may well see a shift in values. Our pastimes of sports and other leisure activities have their place of importance . . . yet clearly, nothing is more essential to our current and future well-being than the education of our children.

Political and Economic Barriers Go Hand in Hand

As citizens, we have a responsibility to exercise our right to vote, in an informed manner, for an educated leader, aware of the complexity of the issues and capable of rebalancing our system.

Many of the roadblocks we see politically could be overcome if our political representatives would put aside the political issues and just do what is right, what is needed, what our children deserve . . . and what they were elected to do. Our party system offers a nice check and balance to our government, but at times it is also a major stumbling block, and an unnecessary one.

The guide for our politicians must come from the experts, from well-done research in interconnected fields that affect the education of our children. The power of our politicians should not be influenced by upcoming elections or any other potential distraction from the seriousness of their jobs. There is nothing more serious, more essential than the education of our youth to prepare them to be able to contribute to our society.

Thus, without compromise:

- Fund our schools all equally. All students deserve a superior education . . . not just a good-enough one.
- Ensure that our schools are safe and healthy places to be.
- Change the policies to allow our children to thrive academically; policies including curriculum, assessment of learning; assistance and support of teachers to become experts in their field, and incentives to encourage our best teachers to work with our most at-risk students are essential.
- Changes must be based upon well-conducted research by experts from the related interdisciplinary fields (both qualitative and quantitative studies are essential) to assure best practices while respecting that individuals vary and that statistically based studies are not the answer for all.
- Understand that assessment practices, as currently required, often do not reflect the skills of our students and interfere with a true education for the twenty-first century based upon curiosity, innovation, problem solving, and collaboration. Furthermore, frequently tests are currently used for rewards, punishments, funding, and accountability issues, none of which the tests were designed to do.
- Support our parents to have access to first-rate early childhood programs, time to be involved in their children's education, medical care for all children, and parenting classes for those in need of such services.

• Support ongoing research in the interconnected domains affecting our educational system.

Economic Barriers

This bring us to the matters that hit us all close to home, the finances of the issues of educational excellence. Because the world is experiencing economic problems, to which our country is not immune, it is now more crucial than ever to understand that penny-wise can definitely be pound-foolish when applied to educating our youth.

The world has changed and is continuing to change, and the United States is falling behind educationally, which ultimately means it will be falling behind economically and in other spheres as well. Without a doubt, our children are the future of our country, the future of our ability to be able to cope in the global economy. If our children are not as well prepared as others, we will continue to decline as others soar.

It is necessary to put aside political differences and allow our nation to regain our academic excellence. Bottom line: what we need educationally involves significant economic support:

• Equity in our schools
• Teachers well compensated for their work
• Monetary incentives to attract the most skilled teachers to work in our most troubled schools
• Support for our future teachers' educational expenses . . . college and graduate-school training as well as for valued beneficial continuing education work
• Safe and healthy school buildings conducive to learning
• Healthy school food programs
• Respect for unions and working together with our policy makers
• Understanding family economic issues and that families need support

Interestingly enough, if we address these needs, many more jobs will be needed, alleviating the unemployment problems and helping to stimulate the economy.

Educational Procedures, Policies, and Logistical Barriers

It should be clear that the problems in our schools are the interaction of problems we see within our country. Most teachers and school personnel are caring, skilled individuals trying to do good work and wanting to see the necessary changes. Yet many are bogged down in too many problems within their classrooms, worrying about test scores and the need to work more than one job to make ends meet. Many also may be poorly prepared for the demands of their jobs with their current educational preparation.

However, we must be careful not to throw up our hands in frustration and declare that we cannot change our whole society, our whole educational system. Deborah Meier (2002) speaks of the power of making small changes, one brick at a time, that lead to larger changes. Each and every one of us must pick up the torch and make the changes we can.

It also is essential to remember that *blame* on any specific factor or group of people—teachers, parents, administrators, or students—is *not productive and in fact is inaccurate*. For we have seen that it is the interaction of multiple factors that has led to the decline and inequity in the academic excellence of U.S. students. Depending upon the lens one looks through, whether it be from a sociological, economic, political, psychological, or educational perspective, it is going to require an interdisciplinary approach to rectify the challenges.

- The twenty-first-century curriculum, changes, and teaching approaches must be based upon solid research from both quantitative and qualitative methodologies . . . and be ongoing and collaborative in nature. The basics in reading, writing, math, science, geography, history, and languages are core, but equally important are the abilities and skills to be creative and innovative thinkers, to be adept at problem solving, to be able to think independently as well as to work collaboratively, and to learn the discipline of research and reflection.
- Without a doubt, our teacher preparation programs must attract the most highly talented students into their programs. The teacher education programs must better prepare our future teachers to conduct, analyze, and implement research to learn in depth about assessment and testing practices, appropriate uses of tests, the limitations of tests, and how to use them effectively in classrooms to better understand each child in order to guide each student effectively.
- Teachers also must keep abreast of current research, attend meaningful ongoing professional development, and collaborate with colleagues in order to assist each student to the fullest.
- Schools need to become safe and welcoming places free from bullies, threats, and toxic conditions. Policies are developed around the needs of the children, not upon the most inexpensive tactic (for example, later class start times for the changing sleep needs of children, healthy food choices, time for exercise and relaxation, time to reflect upon learning without rushing from one class to the next, availability of extracurricular activities, updated resources and technology, etc.).

- The school climate is important in developing healthy schools. In such a healthy environment students are trusted and held responsible for their learning, teachers and administrators are welcoming and approachable, and parents and the greater public are seen as integral parts of the school's community.

Psychological Barriers

Concluding this step with the psychological barriers may be the best ending place, for it is each and every one of us who plays a key role in making these changes. All changes start with one person and grow. Let each one of us be the catalyst for change. In *Barriers to Excellence* we have discovered that we have set up these barriers . . . not intentionally . . . but for misguided reasons. There are ways to overcome these psychological impediments by:

- Being alert to the complex and interconnected issues involved with the barriers preventing academic excellence; understanding that there are likely more barriers to be identified.
- Welcoming discourse, differences, diversity.
- Requiring multiple forms of investigation and assessment. Solely quantitative research approaches are not adequate to understand the complexities of all students; likewise, singular testing approaches are inadequate as well.
- Taking the time to reflect upon our thoughts, emotions, and actions.
- Confronting our anxieties about broader global approaches to learning; understanding that we have developed a barrier related to competition . . . it is really about working collaboratively that is more essential.
- Changing our self-defeating behaviors, including putting off making changes!

Educational excellence cannot have walls. It is more a way of being, allowing students to fully "experience the experience" and to develop their own unique perspectives. It is an education without barriers.

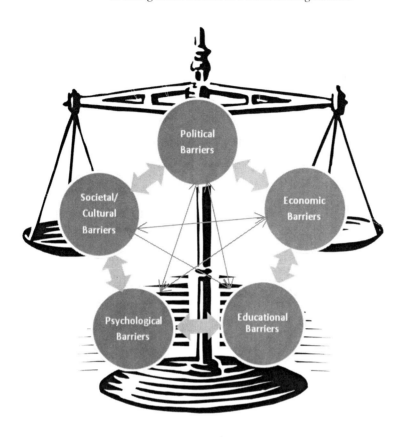

Chapter Ten

Education

Our Key to Future Success

There is no doubt that education is the key to our successful future. But I think you realize by now that our world has changed, and the education of our children needs to change as well for them to be capable of succeeding in our complex global community. Most importantly it will keep changing, most likely at rates even faster than we have experienced in the past two decades.

Education must keep up, adapt, and plan for the future. So what is an education of excellence for the future? Future excellence still requires our students to have a solid knowledge base but also the realization that all knowledge is not knowable. Yes, we do need to develop a solid foundation of reading, writing, math, sciences, history, and the arts (best accomplished through a solid grounding in the arts and sciences).

Even more essential educational approaches are to teach children how to think, how to reason, how to research, how to ask the right questions . . . to grow their intellectual curiosity rather than stifle it, and how to work cooperatively and collaboratively with one another.

This requires a different mind-set allowing for innovation, acceptance, and respect for all others, to realize that alone we cannot make the gains that we might when we work together. Collaboration, cooperation, and working for the common good is what will help the United States regain its position of educational excellence and ensure that we will continue to thrive.

This message seems accurate and is not just my own, but one that I have heard echoed time and time again from faculty members, global interviewees, and many of our top researchers, practitioners, and educational reformers, including the work of Wagner (2008).

The key to excellence brings with it hope for the future, for continued growth and discoveries, for mending the rifts between different countries through global educational collaboration. To learn of others and from others, to bring different perspectives and seek novel solutions is the movement of the future. Just as the Gestalt psychologists have known for some time, we definitely are greater than the sum of our parts. When working as a unit, more is possible than what one can accomplish alone. It truly takes a village, a community, a global community sharing a desire for educational excellence.

For our immediate future and beyond, planning for the future is not easy, but necessary. If we look back just a mere thirty years, so many of our current, everyday technologies that we often take for granted would have seemed like science fiction or even magic that could never really become a reality. Likewise, a few short years into our future it is difficult to foresee what might be possible.

No education would be complete or first rate without understanding our world, all those that inhabit our world, and varying customs, beliefs, and resources and limitations, for true and sustainable educational excellence must involve the totality; to be isolated is to be less, to be incomplete. Real education has no boundaries. Maps have boundaries; education does not. It permeates all barriers; it is about everyone, every place, everything!

So now that we know how to tear down the current barriers to excellence and rebalance our system, we also must begin to think about bridging the divide to global education for excellence, understanding, peace, and sustainability.

No doubt Secretary of State Hillary Rodham Clinton (2009) is correct with her statement: "Science diplomacy and science and technology cooperation between the United States and other countries is one of our most effective ways of influencing and assisting other nations and creating real bridges between the United States and counterparts." However, it will require academic excellence in all domains and collaboration with all our global neighbors for a sustainable, thriving, worldwide actualization.

References and Suggested Reading

Alliance for Excellent Education. (2007). Losing our edge: Are American students unprepared for the global economy? Retrieved September 7, 2008 from http://www.internationaled.org/PISA.html.

Annan, Kofi A. (2001). Nobel Peace Prize 2001: Nobel lecture. Retrieved July 7, 2008 from http://nobelprize.org/eng_lect2001b.html.

Aron , E. N. (1996). *The highly sensitive person*. New York: Broadway Books.

Arriaga, R., & Rangwala, A. (2006). Adolescent storm and stress and identity formation. Unpublished paper.

Arum, R., & Roksa, J. (2010). *Academically adrift: Limited learning on college campuses*. Chicago: University of Chicago Press.

Barber, M., & Mourshed, M. (2007). How the best-performing school systems come out on top. McKinsey & Co. Available at http://mckinseyonsociety.com/how-the-worlds-best-performing-schools-come-out-on-top/.

Carr, N. (July/August 2008). Is Google making us stupid? *The Atlantic.*

Clinton, H. R. (1996). *It takes a village*. New York: Touchstone.

Clinton, H. (2009). Special press briefing on diplomacy and development strategy. Accessed at http://london.usembassy.gov/forpo051.html.

Cottle, T. (1992). Book review of *Savage Inequalities* by Jonathan Kozol. *The Chicago Tribune*, section 14: 5.

Cottle, T. (2001). *At peril: Stories of injustices*. Amherst: University of Massachusetts Press.

Darling-Hammond, L., & McCloskey, L. (2008). Assessment for learning around the world: What would it mean to be internationally competitive? *Phi Delta Kappan* 90(4): 263–72.

Darling-Hammond, L. (2008). Redefining the public role in education. In *Democracy at risk: The need for a new federal policy in education*. Washington, DC: Forum for Education and Democracy, p. 34.

Darling-Hammond, L. (2011). Keep your hand on the plow. Hold on!" (blog). Retrieved January 13, 2012 from http://www.forumforeducation.org/blog/keep-your-hand-plow-hold.

Dede, C. (2011). 21st century learning: Implications for teaching. Presentation at Learning & the Brain Conference, Cambridge, MA.

Duncan, A. (2009). Arne Duncan, U.S. Secretary of Education—Biography. Retrieved May 31, 2009 from http://www.ed.gov/news/staff/bios/duncan.html.

Educational Testing Service. (2010). The black-white achievement gap: When progress stopped. Accessed at http://www.ets.org/Media/Research/pdf/PICBWGAP.pdf.

Finnish National Board of Education. Retrieved July 2, 2008 from http://www.oph.fi/english/frontpage.asp?path=447.

Forum for Education and Democracy. (2008). *Democracy at risk: The need for a new federal policy in education.* Washington, DC: Forum for Education and Democracy.

Forum for Education and Democracy. (2011).

Friedman, T. L. (2005). *The world is flat: A brief history of the twenty-first century.* New York: Farrar, Straus and Giroux.

Gamoran, A., & Long, D. A. (2006). Equality of educational opportunity: A 40-year retrospective. WCER Working Paper No. 2006-9. Madison: Wisconsin Center for Education Research.

Gates, B. (February 2005). Prepared remarks by Bill Gates, co-chair. Available at http://www.gatesfoundation.org/speeches-commentary/Pages/bill-gates-2005-national-education-summit.aspx.

Gates, B. (2008). Bill Gates to Congress: Let us hire more foreigners. Retrieved January 13, 2012 from http://news.cnet.com/8301-10784_3-9892046-7.html.

Gates, B., & Gates, M. (December 20, 2006). Bill and Melinda Gates reflect on need for global philanthropy. Accessed August 15, 2007 from http://www.pbs.org/newshour/bb/social_issues/july-dec06/gates_12-20.

Gates, B., & Mundie, C. (April 19, 2007). Bill Gates, Craig Mundie: Microsoft Government Leaders Forum—Asia 2007. Accessed August 15, 2007 from http://www.microsoft.com/Presspass/exec/billg/speeches/2007/04-19GLF_Asia_Keynote.mspx.

Gates, B. (2008) Retrieved January 13, 2012 from http://news.cnet.com/8301-10784_3-9892046-7.html.

Goodall, J. Retrieved July 6, 2007 from http://www.janegoodall.org/default.asp.

Goodall, J. Preserving, restoring the environment. Retrieved July 6, 2007 from http://www.wsu.edu/goodall/community.html.

Graziano, A. M., &Raulin, M. L. (2010). .*Research methods: A process of inquiry.* Needham Heights, MA: Allyn & Bacon.

Greenberg, M. T. (2006). Promoting resilience in children and youth: Preventive interventions and their interface with science. *Annals of the New York Academy of Science* 1094: 139–50.

Gunzelmann, B. (2004). Hidden dangers within our schools: What are these safety problems and how can we fix them? *Educational Horizons* 83(1): 66–76.

Gunzelmann, B. (2005). Toxic testing: It's time to reflect upon our current testing practices. *Educational Horizons* 83(3): 212–20.

Gunzelmann, B. (Fall 2009). New era/new possibilities: Research-based education for equality & excellence. *Educational Horizons* 88(1): 21–27.

Gunzelmann, B. (2011a). *Hidden dangers: Subtle signs of failing schools.* Lanham, MD: Rowman & Littlefield.

Gunzelmann, B. (2011b). *Hidden dangers to kids' learning: Parent guide to cope with educational roadblocks.* Lanham, MD: Rowman & Littlefield Education.

Gunzelmann, B., & van Loendersloot, T. (2007). Unpublished interview schedule. In Appendix.

Hancock, L. (Sept. 2011). A+ for Finland. *Smithsonian.*

Heyman, J. (2011). Discussion board post, Fall 2011 Psychology 350, advanced research course, Southern New Hampshire University.

Hirsch, E. D. (2006). *The knowledge deficit: Closing the shocking education gap for American children.* New York: Houghton Mifflin.

Holt, J. (1964). *How children fail.* New York: Dell.

KewalRamani, A., Gilbertson, L., Fox, M., & Provasnik, S. (2007). *Status and trends in the education of racial and ethnic minorities.* Washington, DC: National Center for Education Statistics, Institute of Education Sciences, U.S. Department of Education.

Kohn, A. (1992). *No contest: The case against competition .* Boston: Houghton Mifflin.

Kohn, A. (2000). *The case against standardized testing: Raising scores, ruining the schools.* Portsmouth, NH: Heinemann.

Kohn, A. (2004). Safety from the inside out: Rethinking traditional approaches. *Educational Horizons* 83(1): 33–41.

Kohn, A. (December 29, 2008). Beware School "Reformers." *The Nation.* Retrieved January 13, 2012 from http://www.thenation.com/article/beware-school-reformers.

Korpela, S. (2004). Free schooling for all: The Finnish school system supports lifelong learning. Retrieved January 16, 2011 from http://virtual.finland.fi/netcomm/news/showarticle.asp?intNWSAID=41557.

Korpela, S. (2011). A day in the life of Stromberg School. Retrieved January 16, 2011 from http://finland.fi/Public/default.aspx?contentid=162937&nodeid=41807&culture=en-US.

Kozol, J. (1991). *Savage inequalities*. New York: Crown.

Kozol, J. (2000). Foreword to *Will standards save public education?* edited by J. Cohen and J. Rogers. Boston: Beacon Press.

Kozol, J. (2003). Speech presented at Duke University, October 15.

Meier, D. (2002). *In schools we trust*. Boston: Beacon Press.

Meier, D. (2011). Educating a democracy: Standards for the future of public education. Retrieved December 11, 2011 from http://www.bostonreview.net/BR24.6/meier.html.

Merrow, J. (2001) . *Choosing excellence: "Good enough" schools are not good enough*. Lanham, MD: Scarecrow.

Merrow, J. (2004). Safety and excellence. *Educational Horizons* 83(1): 19–32.

Ministry of Education and Culture (Finland). OECD PISA survey. Retrieved September 7, 2008 from http://www.minedu.fi/OPM/Koulutus/artikkelit/pisa-tutkimus/index.html?lang=en.

National Commission on Excellence in Education. (1983). *A nation at risk*. Washington, DC: U.S. Department of Education.

National Sleep Foundation. (2007). Backgrounder: Later school start times. Retrieved August 14, 2007 from http://www.sleepfoundation.org/article/hot-topics/backgrounder-later-school-start-times.

Obama, B. (n.d.). Barack Obama on education. Quotations from On the Issues. Retrieved May 2, 2011 from http://www.ontheissues.org/Celeb/Barack_Obama_Education.htm.

Obama, B. (November 20, 2007). Our kids, our future: Remarks of Senator Barack Obama Tuesday, November 20, 2007 in Manchester, NH. Accessed from http://usliberals.about.com/od/education/a/ObamaEdPlan.htm.

Obama, B. (2008). A world that stands as one. Speech presented in Berlin, Germany. Retrieved July, 25, 2008 from http://my.barackobama.com/berlinvideo.

Obama, B (2008) Change we need: Barack Obama's Speech in Berlin. Retrieved July 25, 2008 from https://webmail.snhu.edu/exchweb/bin/redir.asp?URL=http://my.barackobama.com/page/m/7aba7ee5cc35338f/92xB0B/VEsE/" \t "_blank" http://my.barackobama.com/berlinvideo

Organisation for Economic Co-operation and Development. (2007). Programme for International Student Assessment (PISA) 2006 executive summary. Retrieved September 7, 2008 from http://www.pisa.oecd.org/dataoecd/15/13/39725224.pdf.

Paine, S. L., & Schleicher, A. (2011). What the U.S. can learn from the world's most successful education reform efforts. McGraw-Hill Research Foundation. Retrieved April 10, 2011 from http://www.mcgraw-hillresearchfoundation.org/wp-content/uploads/pisa-intl-competitiveness.pdf.

PISA Program for International Student Assessment (Finnish pages). (2006). Mathematical literacy. Retrieved July 2, 2008 from http://www.pisa2006.helsinki.fi/finland_pisa/results/2006/2006_mathematical_literacy.htm.

Program for International Student Assessment (PISA). (n.d.). PISA 2009 results. IES National Center for Education Statistics. Retrieved May 1, 2011from http://nces.ed.gov/surverys/pisa/pisa2009highlights.asp.

Ratey, J. J. (2008). *Spark: The revolutionary new science of exercise and the brain*. New York: Little, Brown.

Reagan, R. (June 12, 1987). Remarks at the Brandenburg Gate, West Berlin, Germany. Accessed August 15, 2007 from http://www.reaganfoundation.org/reagan/speeches/wall.asp; March 6, 2012 from http://www.archives.gov/historical-docs/todays-doc/index.html?dod-date=612.

Rotberg, I. C. (Ed.). (2004). *Balancing change and tradition in global education reform*. Lanham, MD: ScarecrowEducation.

Rotberg, I. (April 2005). Tradeoffs, societal values, and school reform. *Phi Delta Kappan* 86(8): 611–18.

Sahlberg, P. (2010). *Finnish lessons: What can the world learn from educational change in Finland?* NewYork: Teachers College Press.

Schultz, D. P., & Schultz, S. E. (2008). *Theories of personality* (9th ed.). Belmont, CA: Wadsworth.

Stamm, J. (2007). *Bright from the start*. New York: Gotham Books.

Sternberg, R. Brainy Quote. Retrieved January 10, 2007 from www.brainyquote.com.

Sternberg, R. (2011). Who is really adrift? Accessed from http://www.insidehighered.com/views/2011/02/08/a_critique_of_academically_adrift_and_the_test_behind_many_of_the_findings.

Taylor, S. J., & Bogdan, R. (1998). *Introduction to qualitative research methods: A guidebook and resource*. New York: Wiley.

Tye, K. (October 2003). Global education as a worldwide movement. *Phi DletaKappan* 85(2): 165–68.

UNESCO Education. Accessed September 2, 2007 from http://www.unesco.org/education/en/themes.

UNESCO Institute for Statistics. UIS website. Accessed June 9, 2007 from http://www.unescobkk.org/index.php?id=19.

United States Census Bureau American FactFinder. (2010). U.S. Census Bureau, 2006 population estimates, census 2000, 1990 census. Retrieved March 2012 from http://2010.census.gov/2010census/data.

United States History. Sputnik. Retrieved March 26, 2012 from http://www.u-s-history.com/pages/h1716.html.

U.S. Department of Education. (2008). *A nation accountable: Twenty-five years after a nation at risk*. Washington, DC: U.S. Department of Education. 2008. Available at http://www2.ed.gov/rschstat/research/pubs/accountable.

U.S. Department of Education. (2009). An overview of the U.S. Department of Education. Retrieved January 22, 2012 from http://www2.ed.gov/about/overview/focus/what.html.

U.S. Department of Education. (2011). 2011 International Summit on the Teaching Profession. Retrieved April 12, 2011 from http://www2.ed.gov/about/inits/ed/internationaled/teaching-summit-2011.html.

University of Wisconsin – Madison International Student Services. (2010). *International student handbook*. Retrieved March 7, 2012 from http://iss.wisc.edu/attach/International-al%20Student%20Handbook--Fall%202010.pdf .

Wagner, T. (2008). *The global achievement gap: Why even our best schools don't teach the new survival skills our children need—And what we can do about it*. New York: Basic.

Walker, T. (March 15, 2011). International summit puts best reform ideas on the table. Accessed from http://neatoday.org/2011/03/15/global-summit-puts-best-education-reform-ideas-on-the- table/.

Webster's new world thesaurus. (1990). New York: Simon & Schuster.

Whitehurst, G. J., & Chingos, M. M. (2011). Class size: What research says and what it means for state policy. Brookings Institution, Brown Center on Education Policy. Retrieved December 29, 2011 from http://www.brookings.edu/papers/2011/0511_class_size_whitehurst_chingos.aspx.

Woolfolk, A. E. (2009). *Educational psychology* (11th ed.). Upper Saddle River, NJ: Prentice Hall.

Young, E. (Ed.). (January 2008). Focus on global education: A report from the 2007 PDK summit. *Phi Delta Kappan* 89(5): 349–53.

STUDENT RESEARCHERS

The following undergraduate students at Southern New Hampshire University are involved with the Global Education/Global Voices research project: Ashley Bachelder, Noelle Bourgeois, Joshua Heyman, Heataher Huntington, Angela Jackson, Andrea McMaster, Amanda Meenan Stacie Rivard, Lauren Twombly, and Tina van Loendersloot.

CPSIA information can be obtained at www.ICGtesting.com
Printed in the USA
BVOW031552050612

R4578300001B/R45783PG291148BVX1B/1/P